2.24.93

25.

THE CONCIERGE

THE CONCIERGE

Key to Hospitality

A Training Manual

McDOWELL BRYSON & ADELE ZIMINSKI

John Wiley & Sons, Inc.

New York · Chichester · Brisbane · Toronto · Singapore

The authors gratefully acknowledge the following for providing chapter-opening photographs:

Chapter 1 The Sheraton Carlton Hotel, Washington, DC
Chapter 2 The Grand Hyatt, New York, NY
Chapter 3 The Willard Inter-Continental, Washington, DC;
          and title frontispiece.
Chapter 4 Opryland Hotel, Nashville, TN
Chapter 5 The Palmer House, Chicago, IL
          Courtesy Hilton Hotels Corporation.
Chapter 6 *Courtesy Hilton Hotels Corporation.*
Chapter 7 The Boca Raton Resort and Club, Boca Raton, FL
Chapter 8 The Ritz-Carlton, Naples
          *The Ritz-Carlton is a federally registered trademark of
          The Ritz-Carlton Hotel Company.*
Chapter 9 Ramada Renaissance Techworld, Washington, DC
Chapter 10 The Peabody Orlando, Orlando, FL
          Owned and managed by The Peabody Hotel Group.
Chapter 11 Radisson Hotel, St. Paul, MN
          Courtesy Radisson Hotels International.
Chapter 12 Stouffer Austin Hotel, Austin, TX
          Courtesy Stouffer Hotels & Resorts.
Chapter 13 Doral Tuscany, New York, NY
          Courtesy Doral Hotels & Resorts. Photo: J.J. Perez.
Chapter 14 *Courtesy Hilton Hotels Corporation.*

This publication is designed to provide accurate and authoritative information in regard to the subject matter covered. It is sold with the understanding that the publisher is not engaged in rendering legal, accounting, or other professional services. If legal advice or other expert assistance is required, the services of a competent professional person should be sought. *From a Declaration of Principles jointly adopted by a Committee of the American Bar Association and a Committee of Publishers.*

Library of Congress Cataloging-in-Publication Data

Bryson, McDowell, 1938—
    The concierge: key to hospitality / McDowell Bryson and Adele Ziminski.
        p.   cm.
    ISBN 0-471-52893-5 (paper)
    1. Hotel concierges. I. Ziminski, Adele. II. Title.
    TX911.3.C63B78 1992
    647.94′068′3–dc20   92-2561
                                                         CIP

Printed in the United States of America
10 9 8 7 6 5 4 3 2 1

C · O · N · T · E · N · T · S

Preface   ix

Chapter 1   WHAT IS A CONCIERGE?   1
                History of the Concierge   3
                The European Concierge   4
                The American Concierge   5
                Qualifications of a Concierge   7
                Opportunities for Advancement   8

                Topics for Review and Discussion   11
                Questions   11

Chapter 2   THE HOTEL AND ITS MANAGEMENT   13
                How the Concierge Helps Other Departments   17

                Topics for Review and Discussion   27
                Questions   27

Chapter 3   THE CONCIERGE DESK   29
                Location and Design   31
                Equipment   33
                Storage   34

                Topics for Review and Discussion   37
                Questions   37

Chapter 4   GUESTS: WHO ARE THEY AND WHAT
                WILL THEY ASK THE CONCIERGE?   39
                Guest-History Records   41
                The Six Basic Markets   43
                What Questions Will They Ask?   47
                Guest Education about Concierge Services   51
                Welcome Notes and Phone Calls   53
                Handling Complaints   53

	How to Research Guests and Their Companies	54
	VIPs	56
	Topics for Review and Discussion	59
	Questions	60
	Projects	60
Chapter 5	BASIC TRAINING/ON-THE-JOB TRAINING	61
	Forms and How to Use Them	64
	Confirmation Cards	67
	Logbooks	68
	Phone Manner	72
	Observing Before Acting	73
	Topics for Review and Discussion	74
	Questions	74
Chapter 6	SERVICES PROVIDED BY A CONCIERGE (OUT-OF-HOUSE)	75
	Reservations	77
	Miscellaneous	95
	Topics for Review and Discussion	98
	Questions	98
Chapter 7	SELF-EDUCATION/CONTINUING EDUCATION	101
	Creating Your Own "Black Book"	105
	Some Subject Headings that May Pertain Only to You	158
	Topics for Review and Discussion	159
	Questions	159
Chapter 8	SERVICES PROVIDED BY A CONCIERGE (IN-HOUSE)	161
	General Information and Directions	163
	Mail	163

Packages   164
Escorting Guests to Hotel Restaurants   165
Greeting Guests   166
Escorting Guests to Rooms   167
Building Inspections   167
Room Inspections   167
Showing Rooms   168
Special Amenities to Stock for Guests   169
Equipment and Tools   172

Topics for Review and Discussion   177
Questions   177

Chapter 9   TIPS AND COMMISSIONS   179
                What Should Concierges Be Tipped For?   181
                Commissions   182

                Topics for Review and Discussion   184
                Questions   184

Chapter 10 ETHICS   185
                Guest/Concierge Relationships   187
                What Are the Hotel Rules?   188
                Common Sense and the Golden Rule   189

                Topics for Review and Discussion   190
                Questions   190

Chapter 11 HOW DO YOU BUILD YOUR REPUTATION?   191
                Local Concierge Associations   193
                Clefs d'Or   194
                Public Relations   201

                Topics for Review and Discussion   202
                Questions   202

Chapter 12 CONCIERGE LEVELS 203
The Physical Plant 206
Staff 208
Training 209
Disadvantages of Working on the Concierge Level 213
Special Work Involving Other Departments 213

Topics for Review and Discussion 215
Questions 215

Chapter 13 GETTING YOUR FIRST JOB 217
Resumé Writing 219
Letters From Recruiters 220
Grooming for the Interview and the Job 223
Interviews: How to Enjoy Them and Shine 224

Topics for Review and Discussion 227
Questions 227

Chapter 14 STORIES FROM THE CONCIERGES 229

Index 237

P · R · E · F · A · C · E

This is the first textbook ever written on the intricacies of the concierge profession. In Europe, there has been a long tradition of concierge work, with training taking the form of an extended apprenticeship program. Any formal training has concentrated on the teaching of languages and has been combined with actual on-the-job training.

In the United States, there has been, and is still, very little understanding of the role the concierge can and should play in the daily operation of a hotel or resort. At its best, concierge work is a profession, and the concierge is a quality employee who could be promoted to more important positions. The concierge can be the key to hospitality. Of all the staff in the hotel, he or she is the one who has the most personal contact with the guests. A well-trained concierge can be the reason why guests return again and again, and can embody the quality of service that makes a hotel's reputation.

In order to be a first-class concierge, one must have a thorough understanding not only of the operation of the hotel, but also of the businesses of the outside vendors who provide services used by hotel guests. Americans are not geared to the long wait demanded by the apprenticeship system before they can participate in the job of their choice. A good concierge training program makes it possible for students and employees to go directly into an appropriate job as a valuable and knowledgeable staff member.

This text, which is based on our years of concierge experience, describes the daily functions of the concierge and how to perform them. It also is a valuable tool for students who hope to own their own restaurant, limousine service, or other business that relies on the hotel concierge for referrals. Anyone involved in the hospitality industry can profit from a sophisticated knowledge of who the concierge is, and what he or she does for the hotel and its guests.

We have made every effort to present our material in a user-friendly fashion, and we hope this book will prove to be a valuable supplementary text for the study of hotel operations. We hope also that students will find it easy to read and understand, and will refer to it when they have real jobs in the real world. We assure our readers that the material in this book reflects the situations that we and our colleagues have encountered on a daily basis as concierges.

CHAPTER 1

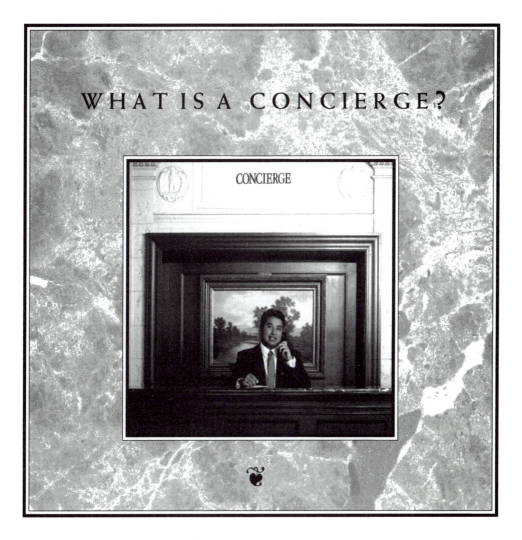

WHAT IS A CONCIERGE?

CONCIERGE

The derivation of the word "concierge" is uncertain. Some theorize that it comes from the Latin "conservus," meaning "fellow slave." Others claim that the first concierge (Comte des Cierges, "Count of the Candles") was in charge of Paris's royal prison, the Conciergerie, where Marie Antoinette was kept before being taken to the guillotine.

Whatever its origin, for the last hundred years or so the term has also been applied to uniformed hotel employees who have their own counter in the lobby. A concierge is a separate entity from the reception staff, room clerks, and cashiers.

History of the Concierge

Until 1936 concierges were not employees of the hotel but independent entrepreneurs who purchased their positions from the hotel and who paid the salaries, if any, of the uniformed subordinates under them. When the legendary Ferdinand Gillet opened Paris's Hotel Scribe in 1926, he had eighty uniformed men and boys in his employ. Now, with the telephone, FAX, and other improvements in communications services, such a large staff is no longer a necessity.

There is very little systematic information available regarding the concierge's job. What there is usually takes the form of magazine articles glorifying the unusual and challenging requests (which tend to be interesting) while ignoring the drudgery. They appear periodically in various slick magazines whose writers focus on the person or persons that particular author thinks epitomize the profession. All have basically said that the concierge is the most important employee of the hotel, and can provide anything one can ask for as long as it's neither immoral nor illegal. This is, of course, slightly exaggerated. All concierges have failures and make mistakes. But the basic idea is sound. The one theme that most writers have emphasized is the difficulty of defining the concierge's job. A concierge can provide a wide range of services for guests while also playing many roles on behalf of the hotel's management. If there is anything a guest needs or has a problem with, the concierge is the person to call. Concierges almost always help, either by taking action themselves or by knowing exactly to whom to refer the guest. In this sense, the concierge provides a backup for such departments as housekeeping and security.

Since the comparison is constantly made, it cannot be overemphasized that the European concierge is the product of a very different system from that of the American concierge. The European concierge's history is much longer, and the training is far different. European concierges also work with a professionalism and a devotion to the job that is almost unknown in this country. Their system of contacts with the purveyors of goods and services has never been equaled here and would be frowned upon by the managers of most American hotels, who might question whether the choice of vendors should benefit the guest or the concierge staff. Sometimes a great deal of both money and favors is exchanged in order to maintain the contacts and provide the services.

The European Concierge

The European concierge system is based on the apprenticeship system—a system that hasn't lasted well in most American businesses. One started at a young age and worked at a menial task, perhaps as a groom. With experience, he or she would gradually be promoted to better and better jobs (chasseur, voiturier, liftier, postier, bagagiste, huissier, assistant night concierge), leading eventually to assistant concierge, concierge, and finally, Chef (Chief) Concierge. The responsibilities of such a job can be considerable and sometimes include managing the entire uniformed lobby staff. Aside from their skills in managing lower-level employees, many of the reigning concierges in Europe have made a practice of learning, on their own, the many facets of fine living in order to understand more of their guests' needs. Some of the newer breed have attended the European hotel schools, which are famous worldwide for training into management positions rather than specifically for concierge work.

All concierges have stories to tell of their fabulous achievements and miraculous accomplishments. While some of these are undoubtedly true, many have certainly been embroidered upon. The daily workload is not always quite so glamorous and actually varies little from country to country. Most requests of a concierge fall into a limited number of categories: restaurant and limousine reservations, theater tickets, directions to almost anything or any place. Handing out maps, tracing lost luggage, and dispensing lots of advice are part of what makes up the overall scene of orderly confusion to be found around any concierge desk.

Incomes, like many of the exploits of the concierges, are known mainly as items of gossip. Although salary data is not easily obtained from European concierges, some have mentioned that a good concierge should earn two to three times his or her salary in tips and commissions. Very few concierges in the United States are paid a high salary, so the addition of tips and commissions will make it comparable only to the income of the average executive secretary.

The American Concierge

The American concierge in most large Eastern cities, like New York and Washington, performs somewhat the same duties as the European concierge, although generally concierges in the United States deal much more with the average business guest rather than with world travelers. Thus, the need for foreign language skills is much less and there are fewer problems of nearby national borders to be crossed by hotel guests. The concierge is seldom in charge of lobby activities and staff, and so American concierges are generally not trained to supervise. They usually report to a mid-level supervisor and cannot function with the degree of independence found in Europe. Because no schools offer formal training in concierge work, and the apprenticeship system is absent in the United States, concierges in pursuit of excellence here lack the opportunity to acquire all the skills of their European counterparts. This may change, as some hotel management begins to perceive concierge service as an edge in highly competitive times. On the other hand, there is always the question of cost versus benefits, and among some of the chains there is a trend toward saving costs by combining concierge duties with other front desk staff.

Having considered the problems of inadequate training, somewhat limited income, and less freedom to perform, one might wonder why the position of concierge has any allure in the United States. The rewards for all concierges, both here and abroad, are primarily those of having done a task particularly well. In a sense, this type of work appeals to the person who truly enjoys doing things for people. It must be pointed out that, considering the job requirements in the United States, the monetary rewards can be considered substantial, but they are seldom the first consideration, and they are frequently limited to the larger cities and then to the luxury hotels and resorts.

Some hotel managers have been known to say that "concierges are born, not trained," referring to the particular motivation of a good concierge to do the job well and to please both guest and management. These managers have hit upon the crux of defining who will make the best concierges. In fact, a frequently heard complaint from American concierges is that the guests aren't demanding enough—the challenges aren't hard enough. This contributes to the large turnover and the general air of dissatisfaction in many American hotels. The concierges keep moving while they try to find those necessary challenges and the accompanying rewards.

A great hotel, regardless of its location, is famous because of its service. All of the hospitality industry's indicators show that although the 1990s may be the decade of downsizing, it will also be a time to emphasize service and to focus on repeat business. A careful survey of industry publications will show that the amount of space devoted to articles on new and better ways to provide service to guests is increasing rapidly. Much of what is being said is not new; it seems new because management has only recently begun to realize the value of proper service as a marketing tool. Basic good service has always been available at the really good hotels. Although many American travelers are willing to settle for what they can get rather than demanding what they really want, there is always a market for the finer things in life. The people who make a profession of knowing about and providing the luxuries available are the concierges, who hold the key to service, repeat business, and subsequent greater profits for the hotels.

Qualifications of a Concierge

Since there is no apprenticeship program in this country, the prior life experience and formal education of the concierge are of paramount importance. Concierges should be mature enough to inspire confidence since their guests may be trusting them with confidential personal matters, important business deals, or plans of a personal nature. The more sophisticated concierges are, the better they will fit in with and understand the needs of their guests. Guests always prefer someone they consider more of an equal, someone who has a knowledge of business and of the demands made upon the guests, because they are traveling in order to conduct business. These guests currently make up the predominant number of people serviced by the concierge. Although large cities may have millions of tourists, they seldom make substantial use of the concierge's talents.

Enthusiasm must be a primary ingredient in the concierge's personality. Whether describing the process of chartering a yacht or selling tickets to a bus tour, the concierge should make the guests feel that they have made a wise decision. One must be able to be cheerful while answering the same questions over and over during the course of the day, and must make each guest feel as though the question is important. The concierge who develops a contemptuous attitude toward tourists looking for the hotel's bathrooms is in the wrong profession.

Organization and efficiency form the basis of effective operations. Since several concierges may work the desk during different shifts, accurate record-keeping is a must. Log books for tickets, limousines, flowers and babysitters must be kept up to date or chaos can result.

Sensitivity to the feelings of others is another important asset. To succeed as a concierge, you have to be constantly attentive to the other person; you have to listen to and look carefully at your guests.

Unfortunately, not everyone who enters the concierge profession possesses the quality of **honesty.** Tales abound of concierges who have pocketed tips meant for others, marked up theater tickets at an illegal rate, or worked "deals" with restaurateurs or limousine companies. Where cash is present, temptation will be also. There is no quicker way of losing the respect of one's colleagues (or one's job) than by being dishonest.

Command of foreign languages is important, but should not be overemphasized. Whereas, if you know several languages, you will always find reason to use them, many concierges function quite well without them. Many foreign business travelers and tourists are very proud of their knowledge of English and relish the opportunity to practice it. In the event of a real communications problem, the hotel staff will normally have employees who speak almost all of the required languages. Many hotels boast anywhere from 40 to 60 various languages among their staff.

Concierges are often on their feet all day long so **stamina** is vital. After work, the concierge might try new restaurants, attend a show, or have a meeting with colleagues. Long days are not uncommon.

Discretion is of the essence. Concierges often know intimate details of their guests' lives. *Tout voire, rien dire* (see everything, say nothing) must be your motto. You will win the confidence of your guests by displaying respect for their privacy.

A warm and friendly personality, the ability to learn how to do research, a knowledge of the business world, and that mysterious psychological need to help people, are the major requirements for the beginner who wants to be a concierge. The rest can be learned through a combination of on-the-job training, formal training in various fields, and, most importantly, an ongoing self-education program.

Opportunities for Advancement

Different types of properties require different types of concierges. Ambition takes many forms, and while one may have heard the legends of concierges who have been in their jobs for twenty-five or thirty years, it does not mean that these professionals are not ambitious. Their ambition has not taken the form of moving up the chain of command or out of the profession; it has taken the form of self-improvement—

always becoming better and more knowledgeable at their jobs. However, one should be aware that this is not the only direction that one's ambition can take. One can also choose to move into other areas of hotel management.

There is no better position from which to observe the operation of the entire hotel than that of the concierge. Concierges are in an opportune position to hear all of the guests' comments about what they like about the hotel and what causes them problems. Working with all of the various departments to solve these problems allows the observant concierge to develop an overview of the inner working of the property that no other single position offers. Concierges share with top management the unique viewpoint of needing all of the departments to function optimally so that they can do their best work. You are not competing with any other department in order to prove your merit; you are actually trying to help every department do its job better. Employees at the reception desk, in the engineering department, the food and beverage areas, and marketing are not so fortunate. They don't share the top management's view of the hotel, and their workload causes them to focus on their own departments almost exclusively.

The concierge's background makes it easy to take the next step: choosing which of the many departments is of the most interest and asking for a transfer in order to learn the intricacies and details of its daily operations. Obviously, there are departments where a previous formal background is essential. You cannot go from being a concierge to being a chef unless you are a qualified cook. You can, however, become a Maitre d' or train to become a room service manager. Housekeeping can also be a desirable next step and, as a concierge, you should already have a good overview of this area because of your experience in making room inspections and showing rooms to guests. If you have worked on a concierge level, you will have worked very closely with the housekeeping management. Moving to the security department is also relatively easy. A good concierge works in tandem with the security officers on a daily basis and has quite a good understanding of the basics of their responsibilities. Since in the process of performing the normal round of duties the concierge functions as a salesperson either for the services within the hotel or those provided by outside vendors, the marketing and sales areas are natural choices and provide a fascinating view of the hotel from an entirely different angle.

The European concept of "once a concierge, always a concierge" does not necessarily apply in this country. Savvy general managers are always looking for employees to promote and train in additional areas. Your chances are based not only on how well you do your current job, but also on the intangibles that mean so much in any industry. The degree of professionalism one shows and the loyalty evidenced toward the hotel and its management are always apparent to those in power. And they count for a lot. Employees who suggest changes instead of complaining about things are noticed favorably, and the way in which they do this contributes to the development of a professional demeanor.

TOPICS FOR REVIEW AND DISCUSSION

1. Discuss the development of the concierge profession from its beginning in Europe to its current situation in the United States.

2. How can one expect to use the position of concierge to train for future management positions?

3. In light of the current position of concierges within the hotels what do you think of their future?

QUESTIONS

1. What has been the role of the concierge historically?

2. How are American concierges different from their European colleagues?

3. How important are language skills in the United States?

4. How does one gain the necessary training to become a concierge?

5. What type of person is most likely to become a good concierge? What personality traits will he or she have?

6. What is the relationship between guests, hotels, and concierges?

7. Do American travelers understand concierges and what they can provide? How are they to learn?

8. Can a concierge be promoted to other management positions? Is this a good place to learn hotel operations?

CHAPTER 2

THE HOTEL AND
ITS MANAGEMENT

It is important for concierges to know as much as possible about the organization of their property and its management. One of the basic tools to use to find out about your company is its Annual Report. The personnel department should be able to provide you with a copy of the most recent annual report, which lists all of the members of the Board of Directors and the top officers of the company. If not, call the treasurer's department at the headquarters office and ask them to mail you a copy. The annual report gives information about all of the top executives and will probably have pictures of them. It will reveal not only their position within your company, but the various other companies with which they may be affiliated. Remember that they are frequently VIPs in their own right as well as being your employer. It is always important to be able to recognize them and to treat them with the same courtesy shown all guests.

The personnel department will probably provide an organization chart for the hotel as part of your orientation program. It is important to know and understand it. If the Personnel Department can't provide an organization chart, make your own. Figure 2.1 is an organization chart of a "typical" hotel. Obviously, the Managing Director or the General Manager is at the top of the pyramid. In a large hotel, their duties are frequently similar to those of the chairman of the board in that they are not so much involved in the day to day operations as in long range planning and overall management. In a small hotel, where they have fewer administrative demands on their time, they probably will be more visible and may play a larger part in daily operations. In such a case, the hotel will reflect their personality in a way that is impossible in larger hotels.

Next in importance are two officers: the Resident Manager, who is responsible for the daily functioning of the property, and the Food and Beverage Manager, who has basically the same responsibility for all of the departments dealing with food. These include room service, banquets, restaurants, and the other areas involved

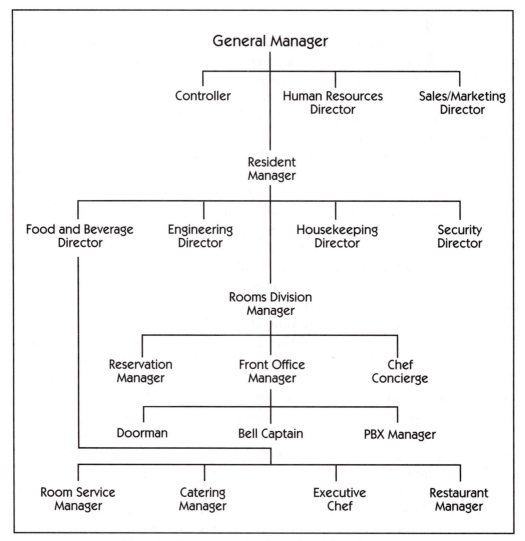

Figure 2.1 Basic organizational chart for a full-service hotel.

with the purchasing, preparation, and service of food and beverages. The Food and Beverage Manager is also heavily involved in the marketing of banqueting functions. This is an enormous job in a large hotel, and he or she has a great deal of autonomy because it is such a specialized area. In many hotels the positions of Resident Manager and Food and Beverage Manager are being combined into one Director of Operations position.

As a concierge, one has little direct contact with the Food and Beverage Director but is very involved with the Resident Manager. In those hotels where concierges are viewed as clerks, they will officially report to the Front Desk Manager. Smart concierges will quickly prove their worth so that they can work directly with the Resident Manager. This does not mean that they have no respect for the Front Desk Manager. It is, again, simply that the concierge and the Resident share the same overall view of the hotel's operation while the Front Desk Manager's main responsibility and interest is in filling the rooms and seeing that the guests are checked in and out efficiently. The Front Desk Manager's first concern will be his or her own department. The concierge will work closely with the front desk in these areas. But when there are other problems, which you as a concierge should make an effort to be aware of, you may find it expedient to notify the Resident who has jurisdiction over the departments that should take action. The concierge who reports to the Front Desk Manager also reports to the Assistant Front Desk Manager.

How the Concierge Helps Other Departments

A good concierge has a unique relationship with all of the management and every department head in the hotel. Your interaction with guests makes you aware of problems or issues which, if not corrected, could lead to guest dissatisfaction and a loss of business. Having established yourself as someone whose judgment can be trusted, you can pass on negative comments in a nonthreatening manner and can head off all kinds of potential problems by calling the person in a position to take immediate action. In this sense, you will often act on behalf of the General Manager

(GM) in order to make everyone look good. If the GM finds out there is a problem, the proper department is already working on it so the department head looks good. The guest is happy because someone not only listened but took action. And the concierge is happy because everything is working smoothly.

Front Office

There are many ways in which the concierge and the staff at the front desk work together. With only a few exceptions these are usually instances where basic knowledge about guests can be shared. Although management does not expect the front desk staff to fulfill the demands made upon a trained concierge, the future holds a role for the concierge as a teacher of all front office staff so that anyone can assist guests with top-notch service.

The services the concierge can provide for the front desk do not involve the mechanics of front desk routine but are the special things that either make the staff look good or are more sales oriented. For instance, when time permits, the concierge can function as a host, leaving the desk to greet returning guests as they arrive and chatting with them as they wait to be checked in. This can be an opportunity to find out what they will be doing in town, what they might want or need during their stay, and to make some suggestions as to things they might be interested in; this is a chance to find out more about the guest, which makes it possible to give them (and subsequently the hotel) better service. The guests love it. So will the General Manager.

Accompanying a valued guest to the front desk is a way of letting the desk clerk know that the guest is of special importance to the hotel. When the concierge introduces a guest by name, it makes it possible for the clerk to find the reservation and to greet the guest by name. A fringe benefit is that the desk clerk may remember that guest in the future. When time permits, you can be useful to the front desk by performing some of the duties their managers would normally do. Room inspections and showing rooms (see Chapter 6) can be a big help, especially when there is a heavy check-in in progress. You might think "why should I help them when they don't lend a hand with my work?" Think about it. You know how to do their work, especially if you have a concierge floor with its own registration desk. But how many people at the front desk are trained concierges? They will be of great value to you when one of your valued guests calls and says he or she needs a room on a night when everybody in town is sold out. When they want to help you they can perform miracles. See that they want to help. You will also need the service of the cashiers, who are part of the front desk staff. Any time that you need to process a "paid out" on behalf of one of your guests you will need to work with the cashiers. They can either make this transaction easy or nearly impossible for you.

Reservations

You will also want to maintain a close and friendly relationship with the reservations department. Although their staff turnover rate is generally much lower than most front office jobs, they may not always recognize favored repeat guests by name. In a sold-out situation, the guests will turn to you for priority treatment, and you can advise the Reservations Manager of the value of your frequent guests. Hotels spend enormous amounts of money cultivating return business, but one sold-out experience can make those guests decide to find a new hotel. Reservations Managers appreciate your alerting them to this sort of situation.

When you are talking to your prospective guests on the phone prior to their arrival, you may very well find out things that the reservations department, for one reason or another, doesn't know. Frequently you will discover that you will need to have a crib or additional bed added to a room. Tell reservations.

Housekeeping

Generally the largest department of the hotel, housekeeping is responsible for cleaning and maintaining the condition of the property. This includes supplying linens, amenities, extra blankets and pillows, if requested, and roll-away beds, which must be delivered and installed. Refrigerators for guest rooms are supplied by housekeeping. Vases for flowers, emergency cleanups when someone is sick in the hallway, and general cleaning of all interior public spaces are in their bailiwick. The latter includes all of the ballrooms and meeting rooms. On rainy days they install the special skidproof runners on the floors. Their employees are also responsible for sweeping and hosing down the steps and sidewalks surrounding the property. As a concierge you will have a great deal of contact with the housekeeping department. Guests will call you, rather than housekeeping, when they are out of amenities, need blankets or roll-away beds, vases for flowers, etc. When you are in any area of the hotel and notice a problem with cleanliness, you will call housekeeping. You will find that you will call them frequently concerning the condition of the public restrooms, one of the most difficult areas for them to monitor. During room inspections, if anything is amiss, you will call them. If a guest reports burned-out light bulbs, call housekeeping or, in some hotels, engineering. When it starts to rain or snow, call housekeeping for the runners to roll over the carpet or floor. If you are alerted that a room has not been made up, they are the ones to call. In some hotels, housekeeping can provide someone to pack or unpack guests' luggage, putting everything neatly into drawers and closets. Housekeeping supplies the robes that many hotels provide for their guests. When a guest wants to buy one, you will call housekeeping, which will provide a brand new robe and handle the charges for it. Housekeeping also functions as the lost and found department. They will sometimes pack items that guests need to ship and are always the first place to call if you have to pack something and require boxes and materials.

If you are working on a concierge floor, you will deal with the housekeeping department in the same way that the front desk does. Since guests will register and check out at your own reception desk, you will rely on your assigned housekeeping supervisor to clean and release rooms for your use. Since all of your guests expect priority service, you will be in constant contact with housekeeping. Their value to a concierge cannot be overemphasized.

Engineering

Another major connection for a concierge is the head of the engineering department. It is to your great advantage to make friends with the engineering staff. While you will be able to help them in many ways, their aid to you can be crucial. Guests with an overflowing toilet won't call engineering, they'll call the concierge. The concierge must get engineering to give this problem top priority. They also handle problems with heating, air conditioning, and television sets. When windows don't work, call engineering. Any problems with electrical connections or outlets that don't work, call engineering. Most importantly, when there is any problem with the elevators, escalators, or revolving doors, call engineering immediately. Guests can have serious accidents involving these areas. When guests are stuck in elevators be sure to advise engineering, then report it to the General Manager and the Resident Manager. If any employees are among those stuck in the elevator, report it to their supervisors so they know where their employees are. We have had the experience of having our General Manager stuck in an elevator for an extended period of time. Report this sort of thing to his or her secretary immediately. It affects the GM's schedule and the secretary will have to rearrange it. Any time there is anyone stuck in an elevator be sure to report it to the security department. This may be a duplication of work done by engineering. On the other hand they have to deal with the actual problem and may forget to alert security. Always report anything to security that might affect the safety of either the guests or your property.

Security

Another one of the people whose assistance is important to the concierge is the Security Director (and department staff). You will be in frequent contact with these people because there is always something happening that requires the aid of, or that affects hotel security. This ranges from lost luggage and injuries to suspected or actual crime. A hotel is a public place, and one never knows what will happen next.

That's part of the excitement about working there, but it's also why one likes to be on good terms with the security department. It's a great comfort to know they are only a phone call away.

Food and Beverage Management

The food and beverage department is comprised of all departments within the hotel where food and beverages are prepared and served. This includes all procurement of provisions and equipment, restaurants, bars and lounges, all kitchens, room service, as well as the catering department. The latter is responsible for all special functions within the hotel. Regardless of whether it is a banquet for thousands in the main ballroom or an intimate gathering in a small meeting room, the catering department will supply the personnel, food, and beverages. Your goodwill can be extremely valuable to the all-important food and beverage department. You will also interact with this department in the setup of food and beverage service in the concierge lounge.

Restaurants

Who is in a better position to recommend eating in the hotel's own restaurants than the concierge? Management expects the concierge to be fully informed about each of the hotel's food outlets: hours of operation, style of food and service, dress code, and so forth. A complex situation has evolved with regard to the food and beverage management and the hotel's concierges that has never been addressed. You need to know about it, and we will discuss it here.

The Food and Beverage Manager and the Restaurant Managers should make a point of treating the concierge just the same as other restaurant owners do. To them the concierge is not just another hotel employee. Concierges can be responsible for a large percentage of a restaurant's business. Some well-known restaurants report that up to 90 percent of their business is sent to them by hotel concierges. Those same concierges can funnel a sizable amount of business into their own hotel's restaurants . . . but most of them don't.

Concierges work very closely with the owners of restaurants in their cities. They are considered to be knowledgeable about food, service, and overall ambience. The importance of the concierge to restaurants cannot be overstated. Savvy restaurateurs recognize that concierges can contribute greatly to their success and seek their support. They do this by actively courting concierges. They invite them to be their guests, to sample their cuisine, to soak up their ambience, and to experience the quality of their service. They have learned the basic lesson that it is easier to sell a product that you know something about, and they see to it that concierges know about their establishments.

Ironically, very few hotel Restaurant Managers extend to their own concierges an invitation to eat (on a day when they are not working) on their own property. Consequently, the concierges may not be able to speak enthusiastically about the hotel's restaurants.

There are many restaurants worthy of recommendation in every city—this is a highly competitive market. Managers who wish to develop business within their own hotels must learn that the concierge is one of the keys to their success. As a concierge, you must have pride in your own property and work with your food and beverage staff to make your restaurants successful and important. Their renown will enhance the name of your hotel, and this will reflect on you and your concierge operation.

Room Service

Depending on the size of your property and the background of your guests, you may find yourself working closely with room service. Naturally, you'll have a copy of their menu at your desk. Non-English-speaking guests frequently will call the concierge with their orders, which you will then transmit to room service. Don't panic about your lack of fluency—this needn't be more complicated than asking "How many?" in the guest's native language, and remembering to suggest beverages. If you've forgotten something (such as asking whether the guest wants the steak rare, medium, or well-done), room service will call you back and ask for clarification.

(You may trust the voice of experience in this!) They'll be most appreciative of your assistance. This is a time when a little homework will come in handy. Learn the necessary phrases so that you can shine.

Birthdays provide another occasion for working with room service. Should a guest not give you adequate notice to have a cake prepared in house, it may be necessary to purchase one outside. Of course, you'll have birthday candles on hand at your desk (see Chapter 8). Obviously, you can't just send the cake up and let the guests fend for themselves. You must notify room service so that they can provide plates, a knife, and forks. This also gives them the opportunity to sell something additional: Would the guest care for a bottle of champagne? Perhaps some coffee? Ovaltine?

Occasionally, a guest will have something that needs to be refrigerated temporarily—this can be anything from medicine to caviar. Your friends in room service will be happy to help you out in these cases. Be absolutely sure that the package is well labeled. You'll have to take it down yourself—guests are not allowed in the "back of the house" or "staff only" areas. Also, local laws on food storage should be checked prior to accepting something to refrigerate.

Banquets and Catering

The banquet and catering department books all private functions in a hotel. These range from small luncheon meetings for six people to dinner-dances for several thousand. Occasionally, due to an oversight, one of these meetings will not appear on the Daily Event Sheet or Reader Board. Consequently, guests attending these functions will not know where to go. What's worse, when they ask you for help you won't know where it is either.

The solution is simple. Call the catering department and ask where the event is to be held. Be sure to advise the front desk staff and the telephone operators. The Food and Beverage Manager, Assistant F & B, and Catering Director should all be wearing beepers. If your call to the catering department doesn't produce the needed information, immediately page one of them. Remember that if an event is not posted it will affect everyone attending the event, not just the guests you are currently trying to help.

Bellstand/Doorman

In some hotels, the concierge supervises the entire uniformed lobby staff, including bellmen and doormen. In others, the bell staff is supervised by the Bell Captain. They are frequently union employees (a concierge is not) who conform to a strict set of rules about what duties they must or must not perform, exactly how much they will be paid for extra services, and their positions in the line to carry bags in order to earn tips. Since their income depends on tips, bell staff naturally prefer to be in the lobby where they can assist guests with their luggage, rather than upstairs making photocopies, delivering messages or flowers, or assisting the concierge in some fashion.

It's extremely difficult to get a bellman to perform a service when there's no tip involved. Even if it is your property's policy that the bell staff deliver messages and FAXes to guests in a timely manner, the bellmen may find ways to avoid being available for this work. If a guest doesn't receive an important FAX quickly, she won't complain to the Bell Captain—she'll call the concierge. If you do not directly supervise the bell staff, there's very little you can do except make this situation known to the Bell Captain or Guest Services Manager. The only way you as a concierge can cope is to do all of the work yourself!

Sales and Marketing

The sales department may sometimes alert you that certain members of a group need special attention. This may range from writing welcome notes to providing foreign language maps. As you work with the groups that have been booked by the sales department staff you will want to be sure to keep the sales representatives apprised of their group members' needs and preferences.

It's up to you to establish your own dependable network within the hotel. When asking for assistance or explanations, convey to your colleagues that you are not looking to take over their jobs, rather that you are trying to understand their procedures so that you can all work together more efficiently. It will make your job a great deal easier and your working environment more pleasant.

TOPICS FOR REVIEW AND DISCUSSION

1. Discuss the usual chain of command within a hotel and how it works.

2. The size of a hotel can make a difference in terms of its "personality." Discuss this and how it affects the role of the concierge.

3. Discuss the role of the Food and Beverage Director and how he or she can work with the concierge.

4. Discuss the concept of the concierge's role in working with other departments to help them with their work.

QUESTIONS

1. Who are the most important management people to the concierge?

2. Which departments will the concierge work with most? Least? Why?

3. What can the concierge do to help other departments?

4. How does the work of the concierge reflect on the overall management of the hotel? How does it enhance the reputations of specific managers?

5. Can the quality of the concierge service in a hotel adversely affect the hotel's image?

CHAPTER 3

THE CONCIERGE DESK

The design and location of the concierge areas within a hotel are crucial factors in terms of the concierge's ability to be useful to both the hotel and its guests. The size of the hotel will determine how many different locations must be provided for concierge service. Since many lobbies are no longer on the ground floor, their location will have an impact on overall planning for concierge services. The number of concierges who must work on the same shift will affect the size of the spaces required and the amount of equipment necessary to enable them to work efficiently. The overall effect that is desired by the owners and architects will also play a major role in the final plan for the various work areas provided.

The physical layout of the small luxury hotel is the most straightforward and the least difficult to describe. The lobby is always on the ground floor or what constitutes the ground floor. A few of these hotels are now located atop multiple-use buildings, but the lobby is still the first floor encountered upon entering the premises.

Location and Design

The front desk will almost certainly be the most dominant feature in the lobby with the concierge area off to one side. While there are still many of the traditional stand-up counters in use, there has been a trend toward having the concierge seated at a table with chairs for the guests to use while discussing their needs. While a table can be very elegant, a counter will usually provide a more efficient system and can be just as attractive. From a practical standpoint, a counter eliminates the problem of guests settling down for a chat while potential customers stand in line waiting their turn. Also, most guests don't want to chat, they want to tell the concierge what their needs are and be on their way. A counter speeds up the transaction of business and increases the concierge's productivity. (It may also give you a psychological advantage to face your guests eye-to-eye, rather than having them tower over you should they choose not to be seated.)

The location of the concierge desk is most important. It must be in a position that enables you to observe everything happening in the lobby, including the entrance doors. If you are responsible for the bell staff, you must be able to see where they are and what they are doing. There must be enough space provided for you to work, and the space, though prominently sited, must be sufficiently out of the way to avoid traffic jams when there are lines of guests awaiting your services.

As mentioned previously, the trend in very large hotels is to relocate the main lobby to one of the higher floors. This means that there is frequently a need for at least partial concierge service on the ground floor while the complete service is relegated to the main lobby upstairs. The same rules regarding placement still apply. Both concierge areas must be immediately apparent to arriving guests. Generally, ground floor concierges will, under these conditions, spend most of their time giving directions to guests who don't know where to go within the hotel or who want sightseeing information, having skipped the main lobby on their way down from their rooms to the street level. Although they will probably not be able to provide full service, these concierges will still be asked to recommend restaurants, provide maps and directions, and to aid the other lobby personnel, such as the security guards, in the pursuit of their duties. They may also be relied upon to police the ground floor lobby to be sure everything is working properly.

A major problem encountered by ground floor concierges as opposed to those on other floors is that of ascertaining where all of the many tour buses are located and seeing that each guest finds the proper one. As a ground floor concierge, it is important for you to keep track of shuttle buses to convention centers and to be aware of their schedules. As convention buses tend to arrive in groups, you will be called upon to work with security in order to ensure the orderly flow of traffic into and out of the hotel so that the lobby is kept clear and functional at all times. You will also rely heavily on the marketing department to apprise you of the various groups in the house and the ones expected to leave and arrive. This can be a very busy and exciting position that will train you to deal with large crowds of people under stress conditions.

Due to the pressures of the workload and the lack of physical space, ground floor concierges are usually not full-service concierges. They will therefore find it necessary to refer guests to the main concierge desk in the main lobby for all of the time-consuming individual requests. For example, as the ground floor concierge, you will not be provided with telephones and reference materials to enable you to call for the many reservations guests request; your time will not permit the record keeping necessary to keep track of guest requirements, and you will have a limited amount of promotional material such as maps and brochures. You will also not be able to leave your post to handle requests for photocopying and FAX transmissions; you must refer guests to the main lobby concierge.

The main lobby, on the other hand, should provide the fullest range of concierge services and must be staffed to handle the quantity of guests who will require them. Again, location of the concierge area is crucial. Guests should not have to hunt for the concierge. You are the one person they should be able to locate with ease.

Equipment

In addition to adequate staff, the main concierge area should be provided with all of the many technical devices and tools to enable the concierges to perform their jobs efficiently and gracefully. For every concierge on duty at any given time, there should be a complete concierge station. You will need telephones, a computer terminal, and all of the hotel forms and clerical tools necessary to perform your duties without interrupting your fellow concierges who are equally busy. You should have your own supply of stamps to sell and your own change supply. Your own telephone books and up-to-date card files for frequently called contacts are also essential.

The things that can be shared should be. It takes up less storage space. For example, sightseeing brochures can be arranged against a wall where the guests can browse through them without having to approach the concierge until they have specific questions. It's more convenient for the guests and reduces the concierge's workload.

The desks and/or countertops provided should be large enough to work on without being so large that there is a gulf created between the guest and the concierge.

This is supposed to be a *personal* service, and guests shouldn't have to shout their requests in order to be heard.

A concierge needs a supply of reference materials and handouts for guests. Following is a list of the basics:

- ❏ **Reference materials:**
  Log books   Telephone books
  Official Airlines Guide   Zip Code Directory
  Hotel and Travel Index   Who's Who in America
  Who's Who in Business   Hotel Personnel List
  Operations Manuals
- ❏ **Brochures and handouts**
- ❏ **Maps (in various languages):**
  Street
  Subway
  Bus
- ❏ **Tour brochures**
- ❏ **Hotel brochures and advertising**

Storage

Storage is probably the worst problem. Architects and managers seldom know what it is they are providing space for and what the sizes of the various things are. A sample of storage requirements is:

- ❏ **Forms:**
  In-house forms
  Delivery services (Federal Express, etc.)
  Tour reservation books

- **Stationery:** all kind and sizes.
  (There is a large range of sizes in envelopes.)

- **Packing supplies:**
  String and twine
  Various types and sizes of tape

- **Special amenities:**
  The concierge needs a locked storage area for amenities that guests frequently forget to bring with them and usually need when all stores are closed. We'll provide a complete list in Chapter 8. Generally, these include sewing kits, bow ties, regular ties, shirt studs, tie clips, scissors, combs, toothbrushes, etc.

- **Luggage:**
  Even with a bellstand available, guests will ask if you will keep their luggage for "just a few minutes." Since it's frequently impossible to refuse without antagonizing a guest, space must be provided, although it seldom is.

- **Flowers:**
  Until such time as flowers can be delivered to a guest, they must be stored in a secure space.

- **Guest mail boxes:**
  In some hotels the front desk takes care of guest mail. In others, however, it is the duty of the concierge. Boxes must be provided that are large enough to handle the largest envelopes a guest is likely to receive.

- **Outgoing mail:**
  Each concierge area needs a box in which to store outgoing mail until it can be taken to the mailroom. Otherwise it ends up in various places and is frequently lost.

❑ **Locker space:**
Since the hotel's employee lockers are too small for the use of concierges, who have their uniforms, personal clothes (frequently formal because they have to attend functions on behalf of their hotel), and their personal collection of reference books and materials, the thoughtful hotel will provide locker space of adequate size for them. Concierges also require locked space within their areas for personal belongings and reference materials.

The actual design of all hotel space, including that of the concierge, is done by architects or interior designers. It is their duty to understand how a concierge works and why. Their experience with other construction projects may give them knowledge that can be transferred to the hotel's design, and they will be aware of the efficiency of providing the proper tools adjacent to the person using them. Sending FAXes and making photocopies occupy a great deal of the concierge's time. The necessity of your going several floors away and waiting in line while the General Manager's secretary runs a 500-page report can seriously undermine the image of the hotel. This type of equipment needs to be placed near the concierge, preferably behind the counter. It is no longer a special service provided for guests; it is as commonplace as the telephone.

Concierge levels or floors have become very popular with the guests who frequent the large hotels. Since to a great extent they function as hotels within hotels, they have their own design requirements. Chapter 12 is devoted solely to an indepth examination of this highly successful phenomenon.

TOPICS FOR REVIEW AND DISCUSSION

1. Discuss the positioning of the concierge operations with regard to traffic flow and the front desk location.

2. Discuss the advantages of being assigned to the ground floor in a large convention hotel.

3. Discuss how the positioning of equipment can affect the work and efficiency of a concierge.

QUESTIONS

1. Where should the concierge desk be located? Why?

2. Which departments will the concierge work with most? Least? Why?

3. What is different about the duties of the ground floor concierge in a large hotel?

4. What must the architect consider when designing a concierge desk or concierge work area?

5. What should concierges have at their work stations?

6. What are the advantages of working at a standup counter as opposed to a sit-down desk?

7. What tools or materials can be shared by concierges who work the same shift?

GUESTS: WHO ARE THEY AND WHAT WILL THEY ASK THE CONCIERGE?

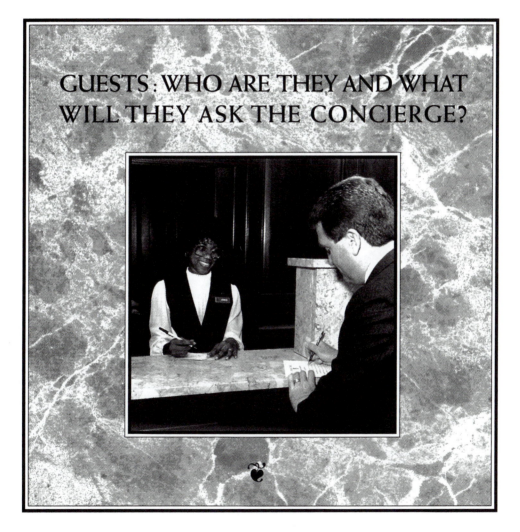

4

Guests are the most important people who enter our hotel. They are here because of the many services we provide and will satisfy their needs and desires either with us or with one of our competitors. Guests are not an interruption of our work—guests *are* our work. Their wish should be our command!

Guests are the reason there are hotels and resorts. They are, therefore, the reason concierges have jobs.

Guests are not a cold statistic—they are flesh and blood human beings with feelings and emotions, their own likes and dislikes, biases and prejudices.

Guests can be anyone on the face of the earth—royalty, heads of state, rock stars, movie stars, construction workers, and school teachers all travel and are someone's guest. Naturally, their needs vary considerably based upon who and what they are.

Guest-History Records

A guest history can be one of a concierge's most valuable tools if properly kept and maintained. You will find, however, that guest histories are seldom kept up-to-date by the majority of concierges and are rarely used. You will also find that these concierges know very little about their guests. Don't follow their example; the more you know the better off you will be. The information you will find most useful to you is:

- ❑ Name of guest
- ❑ Occupation
- ❑ Addresses (offices and homes)
  Know where you can contact your guest at all times. You never know when you might need to.
- ❑ Telephone numbers (offices and homes)

❏ **Secretary's name**

A good secretary is more likely to have access to the boss than anyone, including his or her spouse. If you need to reach the boss, speak to the secretary first. Should the boss not be available, you may handle most of the arrangements with the secretary. Be sure the secretary understands who you are and what you are trying to do. Like everyone else, secretaries appreciate being called by their names.

❏ **Spouse's name**

❏ **Names of children**

❏ **Preferred hotel rooms**

Many repeat guests have preferences for certain rooms. This may well be simply a personal preference having nothing to do with either price or decor. You may also like to keep a list of your guests' favorite hotels in other cities as well as the name, of the concierges there so that you can coordinate their trips.

❏ **Favorite restaurants**

You will find it helps you with making reservations if you can remind the Maitre d' that your guest has been at the restaurant before. When making reservations at these restaurants for your frequent guests, it is a nice touch to remind them of the Maitre d's name so that they can greet him or her properly.

❏ **Special interests**

Knowing about guests' special interests enables you to watch for things they will want to know about when they visit your city. If you know that a guest enjoys visiting auction houses, for example, you may want to call his secretary to mention a particular sale and ask whether he is aware of it and is planning to attend. If so, it gives you the opportunity to make all the arrangements for him, including reservations in your hotel. Guests are invariably delighted that the concierge took the time and the initiative on their behalf. You will be amazed at the wide range of interests your guests have.

❑ **Special information**

There are all kinds of seemingly unrelated bits of information that you can accumulate that will enlarge the picture you have of your guest and enable you to seemingly perform miracles. It's helpful to have odd bits of information—if a guest is allergic to feathers, you can call housekeeping and remind them to replace the pillows with foam rubber before the guest arrives.

The Six Basic Markets

There are six basic markets from which guests come:

1. Conventions
2. Tour groups
3. Small group meetings
4. Airline personnel
5. Permanent guests
6. Transients

Guests attending conventions are there to work. Because of this, the demands upon your skills and patience will be considerable. It is important that you work with your hotel's Director of Convention Sales. The director can supply you with information about any individual convention group staying at your property. This will include such things as the names of the leaders of the group, the VIPs and their room numbers (a vital piece of information), the name of their charter bus company, with contacts, and the schedule of events they may have planned within the hotel. The information will also include how many attendees are expected at various events, which will enable you to gauge your workload and to anticipate traffic flow through public areas. You will have many more requests for reservations (limos, restaurants, theaters, etc.) as well as more demands on your time in terms of directing traffic within the hotel. You should be aware that during conventions everything that can happen in a hotel environment is compressed into a microcosm. Lots of things go wrong, and you will constantly be called on for help. People may get lost, drink too much, or have accidents. Occasionally guests report thefts, and there is the occasional fight. You will work closely with the security department because you are a primary representative of management. These things are not normally talked about, but they are one facet of the hotel business and they do happen. How you handle emergencies will help to determine the course of your career. It's a lot of fun but also lots of hard work. Your performance during conventions is invaluable to your hotel and helps to generate return business. Guests in this market can be further broken down into:

1. *Trade show exhibitors and attendees.* Exhibitors are normally sales and promotion professionals who spend a great deal of their time traveling to various shows. Consequently, they will usually have considerable experience in dealing with both convention centers and hotels. In addition to their personal hotel rooms, they frequently will use hospitality suites for entertaining on a more intimate scale. These guests are generally well acquainted with the full range of services they can expect and will take advantage of them. Exhibitors will have boxes, bags, and armfulls of material that they are moving back and forth between the center and the hotel. They require transportation for this material. In addition to the regular buses, they may need limos, radio cars, station wagons, or small buses of their own. Be prepared to analyze their needs and to make suggestions. They will make great demands on your ability to receive advance shipments of materials prior to their arrival at your hotel as well as to pack and ship materials back to their offices when the convention is over. Emergency transmission of both mail and packages in and out of the hotel will also be a priority item.

2. *Educational groups.* Groups of professional educators are among the most difficult and challenging groups you will encounter. Because they are accustomed to being in control of their teaching environment, they frequently find it hard to rely upon aid and advice from a concierge who looks like he or she might be one

of their students. Their travel budgets are usually not lavish and prevent them from taking advantage of exotic or expensive treats. If you keep in mind that you are not a student but a professional with information of value to them, they will respond immediately, and it will be possible for you to use your contacts to arrange less expensive but high quality alternatives.

3. *Medical and scientific groups.* These groups share many traits with educational groups. They are used to being in charge; they are used to being in a controlling situation; they are used to demanding something and getting it in their daily work. They are also very intelligent and can be reasoned with. Because of their status and the demands of professional entertaining, you can expect to make many reservations at the best restaurants and to provide limousines for transportation. The latter is not because of their need for ostentation, but because there will normally be too many of them to fit into a taxi.

4. *Fraternal organizations (Shriners, Elks, Moose, etc.).* Regardless of the fine work they may do at home and their contribution to society in general, these groups are notorious within the hotel industry for their ability to be disruptive and to cause damage. They are generally very well organized and will have most of their activities planned before they arrive.

Members of tour groups will not have booked their stay directly with your property. This will have been done through the tour company, for example, Dailey-Thorpe, Kuoni Tours, among others. Since most tour groups arrive, dine, go to the theater, go sightseeing, and depart together, their needs will generally be taken care of by their tour operator.

Small groups (generally under 20 rooms) arrive for a specific event. This can be anything from a sales meeting to a wedding. Most of their needs will be handled by the banquets and catering department.

Airline personnel are in town to rest between flights. They almost never ask the concierge anything.

Permanent residents and transient guests are the most likely to ask the concierge to provide services and are a source of frequent tips. Transients can range from a couple in town on a discounted "getaway" weekend to the South American widow who always spends two months of "The Season" in your city. Of all the categories of guests, they are the mostly likely to return to a hotel because of superior services rendered.

The size and nature of your property will determine whether most of your work will be with transient guests, conventioneers, or permanent residents.

It is the concierge's job to satisfy guests while winning their respect, interest, admiration, and goodwill by the quality of service provided. This will serve to invite their continued patronage—the "repeat business" that is the bread and butter of the hospitality industry. Every guest, from the sophisticated traveler to the first-timer, responds to friendly, personal service. Don't forget the four basics of guest relations:

1. *Greet the guest.* Begin with "Good morning" (afternoon, or whatever) before asking, "How may I help you?" If it seems appropriate, this is the time to use your language skills to help foreign guests feel welcome.

2. *Use the guest's name.* But remember that while this establishes a bond between you and your guests and helps to establish them in your memory, there are also times when guests may find overuse of their names to be too familiar.

3. *Maintain eye contact.*

4. *Smile.*

If you are fluent in the guest's language, speak it. Don't be shy. Your guest's relief at being able to communicate in his native tongue will far exceed any judgments about your possible grammatical errors.

Guests to whom you have been particularly helpful in the past will seek you out on their next visit. But it is in your best interest (and the hotel's) not to wait for them to find you. At the start of your shift, you should read the Arrivals Report. This will list all expected arrivals. When you find the names of guests you know and have helped on previous visits, refer to your Guest-History File. This is where you will record all of the data about your important guests. It should list all of the things you need to know about them. Refresh your memory concerning their favorite restaurants, and so forth, and write a brief welcoming note to them. Leave the note at the registration desk where they will receive it when they check in. You may follow this up with a phone call after they arrive. Due to time constraints, you may find it difficult to prepare notes in which case you can rely exclusively upon the phone call. Check your computer terminal periodically to see whether they have arrived.

Guests will treasure you for more than just your information and connections; they want someone whom they can trust, someone they can turn to with their problems. It's a big responsibility but enormously rewarding. Many guests develop a relationship with a particular concierge and use him or her exclusively for all their communication with the hotel. If guests want room reservations, they'll call the concierge. If they have a complaint, they won't call the General Manager, they'll call the concierge. Every time the phone rings, it's an opportunity for the concierge to establish this sort of relationship with a guest. The importance of a good phone manner is discussed in Chapter 5.

What Questions Will They Ask?

Over the years, concierges have earned the reputation of being "people who know everything," and guests will put this to the test. One of the most enjoyable things about working as a concierge is that every day presents different challenges—the work is never boring because you never know what people are going to ask. For starters, guests will ask all of the questions you would need to ask if you were traveling to a strange place and staying in an unknown environment: where are the best restaurants, what are the most important sightseeing attractions, is it safe to take the subway? Fortunately, a great number of questions fall into a limited number of categories. This means that even with a limited amount of knowledge one can handle most questions. Being left alone at the desk can be terrifying the first time, but, if you have done your homework, you should relish the opportunity to shine.

On the other hand, you will get unusual questions sooner or later, and you must be able to deal with them. To a great extent, it is the way you handle these unusual questions that will establish your reputation as a quality concierge. You will also find that these are the high points in your workday and are what make the job both exciting and challenging.

Most guests who pose an unusual question or make a complicated request will not require an immediate answer. A sincere "You know, I've never been asked that before. Please let me investigate and get back to you," will assure guests of your intention to assist them. Just be sure that you are true to your word and really follow through.

Let's say that you are really stumped by a request. Where's the first place to turn? Your colleagues: both your fellow concierges and the staff in other departments. Don't fall into the trap of thinking that only concierges have information. The doormen and bellstand staff are storehouses of knowledge about the city and various methods of transportation. Don't rely, however, on their information about restaurants. If you need help with restaurants call the Director of Food and Beverage, the Chef, the Restaurant Manager or the Maitre d'. Food is their business. They will be glad that you recognized their expertise and will be flattered that you came to them with a question.

If your fellow concierges in the hotel are available, they are the logical people to ask for help. If you are working alone, don't forget the concierges in other hotels. Most large cities have concierge organizations, and their monthly meetings provide a wonderful opportunity to become acquainted with other members of your profession. You will find that concierges have a great willingness to help one another. Call one of your more experienced colleagues and inquire whether she has ever dealt with this sort of problem before. Perhaps she can steer you in the right direction.

If she can't, ask yourself, "To whom would this information be important? Who would want to know?" Think about your friends and relatives . . . do they have any special hobbies or unusual interests?

For example, some British guests arrive and ask you for the football (soccer) scores of today's matches. Don't panic. Ask yourself who else would be interested. The sports section of the newspaper and Reuters, the international news wire service, would be possible solutions. Incidentally, you will find that when you call a place like Reuters and ask for assistance, their staff will invariably be delighted to help. Finding the answer is like being involved in a mystery, and people very much want to join in the fun of finding the solution. Try to find out where this type of information is readily available, in preparation for the next time you are asked a similar question. For instance, why call the newspapers if there is a sports hotline number to call that has a recording that announces the scores of sporting events?

You may find that the reference librarian at your local library can assist you, but don't count on it. Fiscal cutbacks in city budgets limit library staffs, curtail their hours, and increase their workloads. It can be difficult getting information in a timely manner. They also have only limited knowledge of the type of material you will need.

Giving Directions

Guests will ask for directions to museums and sightseeing attractions, stores, and restaurants; instruction on how to use public transportation; the location of the nearest cash machine; and a wide range of other topics for which the information must be at your fingertips. You will also be asked for directions within the hotel ("Where's the rest room?" is probably the most frequently asked question). Have the Daily Event sheet handy so that you know what functions are taking place in the various meeting rooms. To be an effective concierge you must develop the ability to give clear, concise, information that your guests can understand and remember.

Unless the place in question is within a few blocks, we recommend immediately pulling out a map, marking the hotel's location with an X, and tracing the route to the destination. This will prevent any misunderstanding. Should guests wish to take public transportation, explain the fares, verify that they have exact change or know how to buy the needed pass or token, and write out the directions clearly: "Walk to Sixtieth and Fifth and take the N train downtown to Times Square."

Study your city's subway and bus maps (which you should also have on hand for guests) so that you'll know the easiest way to the most popular destinations.

Develop your own shortcuts for dispensing information quickly and accurately. For the sake of speed in assisting its thousands of guests, the Hyatt Regency in Chicago has cards printed with directions to major attractions, both for public transportation and driving. This sort of thing can save you untold time and headaches.

Reservations

Guests will ask both for information about restaurants and for dinner reservations. Limousines, theater tickets, airline tickets, tour reservations, reservations at other hotels as they continue their travels, and a variety of other related requests will be made of you. Be aware that these questions will be asked: they are part of the overall picture of who the guest is. In Chapter 6 you will find complete information about how to deal with these questions.

Mail

You will almost certainly be asked many questions about mail: the cost of stamps for mail to various destinations in the world; the address and hours of the nearest post office and the main post office. Guests will ask if you are holding mail for them as they arrive and will ask you to forward mail to them when they leave.

General Information

Guests will ask for all sorts of general information, such as: "When's the last Mass at St. Gregory's?" "How late is Marshall Field's open?" "Where can I buy some cheap luggage?" "Is it safe to walk from here to the theater?" We recommend giving the guest a map and highlighting the areas to be avoided. Whether or not the public transportation in your city is "safe" is a judgment call to be made with caution. If there is any doubt in your mind, recommend that the guest take a taxi.

Guest Education About Concierge Services

Guests fall into two broad categories: those who are familiar with a concierge's services and know exactly what to ask for and those to whom this is a novelty. Don't confuse this issue with the problem of guests who can't figure out what plans they want to make. These people may very well understand the things a concierge can do for them and be using you to sort out their own decision-making problem.

The most demanding guests are often the easiest to accommodate. They will tell you exactly what they want and when they want it. Compare Guest A who says, "I need a table for four at Tropica on Tuesday at 8:30, plus a limo to take us there," with Guest B who confesses that his "party of four or maybe eight wants to go out tonight but they're not quite sure what they're in the mood for." Guest A obviously knows exactly what a concierge can do for her. Guest B needs the best of your "suggestive selling" techniques to help him narrow down his choice between a "quiet and romantic" bistro, a "lively and sophisticated" pasta palace or yet another place with an "unparalleled view." Guest B may also understand that the concierge can help him. But he is much more difficult to satisfy because you have a large number of choices available for him, and he has given you no idea of where to start.

You have opportunities for education in both instances. Guest A should be reminded that there is a minimum charge for limos and that you will have the limo wait to bring them back to the hotel after dinner. Since she has asked specifically for a limo, you need to ask if she wants a standard size or a stretch, a much longer and more expensive car. Guest B offers an even bigger opportunity to display your talents. Since he can't seem to narrow down something as basic and important as how many will be in his party, you must assume the worst (the greatest number) and insist that he advise you later about the correct number. You will need to suggest restaurants where you can book tentatively for the larger number and lower the number if necessary. You must tell the Maitre d' of the restaurant what the situation is so he or she can help you. One of the things that will help you is knowing more about the purpose of your guest's entertainment and who his guests are to be. If it is to be an opportunity for informal business discussions, don't suggest noisy nightclubs or the theater. Suggest a quiet restaurant where it is possible to hold a discussion. On the other hand, should your guest be entertaining friends or colleagues who want a big night on the town, use the nightclubs or theater. For a really complete social evening in New York, for instance, you might arrange for the following: a stretch limo to pick your guests up at the hotel and stay with them for the entire evening; pretheater dinner at Marie-Michelle or another "name" restaurant; the theater or a performance at Lincoln Center at 8 o'clock; after the theater, a quick drive to Forty-second Street to Chez Josephine for a small supper while watching the show and listening to their famous jazz piano players; back to the hotel in the wee hours of the morning. It's a great evening and very expensive.

You must size up your guests before making suggestions. But you must also start somewhere. Suggesting something will break the ice. It gives your guests something concrete to like or dislike. The price of such an evening will provide them with material to think about. They have also just learned a lot about the range of services you can provide. Even if they don't use anything you suggest, they know a lot more about the concierge. By the time you have either arranged for their evening or not, you will also have had opportunities to discuss with them their reasons for visiting your city and hotel and will have had the chance to ask if you can help with other things such as airline reservations or confirmations and their method of transportation to the airport. Don't forget to suggest that the next time they are coming to your city, they call you in advance so that you can arrange for their activities while they are your guests.

Welcome Notes and Phone Calls

Another practical way of introducing yourself to guests is by sending them welcome notes. Frequently, a General Manager will ask the concierge to send notes to important members of a group. Sometimes, the sales department will alert you that someone needs special attention. Sometimes, a concierge whom you have never met will call and tell you that Mr. X. is a special guest of hers and ask that you take care of him. In any of these instances, a brief note introducing yourself and offering your services makes the guest feel especially coddled. If English is not the guest's native language and you feel comfortable writing in whatever language it might be, do so. This can overcome guests' hesitation about approaching someone by whom they might not be understood. In many cases, the guests won't need you to do this. Nevertheless, they will remember this gesture; it sets them apart from the hundreds of other guests who have checked in that day.

You may prefer to telephone guests just after their arrival to introduce yourself and your services. You don't want this to be a long interruption of their unpacking—rather a short, "I'm just calling to check whether there is anything I might do to make your stay with us more enjoyable. Do you need dinner reservations, a limousine, or perhaps theater tickets? Please don't hesitate to contact me."

Handling Complaints

We live in an imperfect world, and sometimes things go wrong. Laundry gets delivered to the wrong room. Room service is slow. The restaurant you recommended for a special occasion has changed owners, and the food was awful. When there is a problem, guests naturally turn to the concierge for a solution.

It's important to distance yourself psychologically from the complaint—it's not a personal attack on you, it's a plea for help. Don't take it personally. There are a few basic rules to remember when dealing with guests' complaints:

1. *Listen.* Don't interrupt or you'll just make matters worse. Let your guest fully explain what has happened.

2. *Restate the complaint to the guest in your own words* to be sure that you have understood completely. Be sympathetic. Show that you understand your guest's point of view—don't be afraid to use phrases like, "I understand how frustrated you must feel."

3. *Promise to find out what's happened* and then *do it.* But don't promise what you can't deliver.

4. *Get back to the guest promptly,* even if you have to give him bad news. If the ironing machine ate three of his shirts, waiting to tell him won't make them magically reappear.

5. *Offer a solution.*

6. *If the guest is still unhappy,* suggest to management that they make a small conciliatory gesture. A bowl of fruit accompanied by a personal note from the General Manager can turn dissatisfied guests into ardent fans.

In the unfortunate event that you are faced with a "screamer," someone whose temper is just boiling over, get the guest out of the lobby to a private place. You don't want other guests to be unfavorably influenced. If you're afraid the irate guest might get violent, call both Security and the Resident Manager.

How to Research Guests and Their Companies

Very few concierges ever research guests to find out who they are and why they are important. But you should know how to do it in case you get really interested in the people in your Guest-History File. It can also be useful to know something about your guests' background when asking for some preferential treatment for them. When you mention to a Maitre d' that your guest is the president of Mitsubishi or the CEO of the company that owns both Tiffany's and Jiffy Lube, you will find that doors suddenly open. Researching a guest is no more difficult than researching a term paper—probably a lot simpler. For one thing, you decide when you know enough.

If your library uses the Dewey Decimal system, you'll find reference material starting at 920 and continuing through 928. Here are some of the more useful sources:

Annual reports of companies. The yearly reports issued by companies can be a storehouse of information about their executives as well as telling all about the business they are in. Usually the list of company officers and the Board of Directors is to be found in the back of the report. Frequently the pictures in the body of the report will show the officers at work, which will give you an idea of their corporate environment. This in turn tells you a lot about the accommodations and the level of service they will expect from a hotel. From the furnishings you might be able to determine interests in art or other collectible items.

Financial magazines. If you can find a writeup about someone in a financial magazine it will probably be a comprehensive one. Their articles tend to be well researched and frequently include material from interviews, giving an in-depth picture of your guest. Since you are interested in guests, not magazines, there is no point in providing a list of magazines. Go to your library and use the *Reader's Guide to Periodical Literature.* Look for your guests' names in the subject index and you will find a list of the magazines containing articles about them.

Society magazines. You may occasionally find that *Town & Country, Vogue,* or *European Travel & Life* will feature an article on one of your guests. These generally include a lot of pictures and will give you an interesting glimpse into his or her lifestyle.

Wall Street Journal. Indispensable for keeping track of important happenings in the business world.

Who's Who in America. There are a variety of *Who's Who* volumes, each of which concentrates on a different group of VIPs. The name of the volume tells it all. Since most of your guests are probably Americans it makes sense to look here first. This is the most general volume for this country but there are also books devoted to specific professions. For instance, if you know that your guest is a doctor, you will want to consult *Who's Who in Medicine*. The books are published annually and arranged alphabetically. They give brief but comprehensive data.

Who's Who International. Here is your basic reference tool for international travelers. If you find you want more data your next step will probably be the *Reader's Guide to Periodical Literature*.

Current Biography. Published yearly by the H.W. Wilson Company, *Current Biography* gives long, rather gossipy writeups on celebrities from every walk of life.

VIPs

Although in the hospitality business every guest is a very important person, there are still those to whom we try to render extra service because of their special status in the world. Film stars, famous musicians, and royalty immediately spring to mind, but there are lots of other examples. Businesspeople who have worked their way to the top are often thought of as the royalty of this country. Chairman of the Board, President, Chief Financial Officer, and a number of other titles carry a mystique that grows in direct proportion to the size and prestige of their company. High ranking military officers, politicians, society figures, and just plain rich people often fall into the VIP category. And then there are the people who have made their names in the professions: scholars, doctors, and lawyers of note.

How Are They Different?

One begins to understand more about the reception and service due to VIPs as one thinks about why they are VIPs. Most of these people have worked hard to reach prominence and it has affected their lifestyles. Most of them have personal staffs, employees, bodyguards, and advisers who provide for their needs in various ways. They are used to being taken care of. It is necessary, in many cases, if they are to have time to get their work done.

How To Treat Them

VIPs are in your hotel for a reason . . . usually having to do with work or some business they must take care of. Film stars may be there for a movie they are working on or for a personal appearance of some type. Businesspeople are normally having meetings or attending conventions. At times, even VIPs take time out for a vacation. Regardless of why they are staying with you they deserve the same attentive service you bestow upon all of your guests. Pay attention to how they respond to you and to others with whom you see them interacting. You will quickly see how much attention they want and what types of things they value.

Don't be nervous. You are dealing with them as a professional—not as a starstruck child. Do not be overly subservient or too pushy. Be yourself. By the same token, don't berate yourself if the sudden appearance of a celebrity gets you flustered—they're used to having this effect on people. Years of dealing with the public have taught us that some of the most important people are also some of the nicest.

What Special Things Will They Want?

Privacy seems to be one of the major considerations of people who live in the public eye. This was pointed out by one guest in a major hotel who finally said that he appreciated all of the attention he was getting from the staff, but that he couldn't get any work done if he had to keep answering the door. If you find that your VIPs are getting a lot of attention, you might ask them if they would prefer to have things handled differently in order to give them more privacy. You will find that VIPs' lives are fairly structured. They have schedules of meetings or activities that are the real reason they are with you, and their lives revolve around them. They may very well have some of their own staff with them to handle all their requirements. You may find that you never deal with VIPs directly but get a lot of requests on their behalf.

A VIP who is in town on business will probably receive a great many FAXes and Federal Express packages, and these should be delivered without delay. People who have risen to the top of their profession didn't get there by being disorganized and not planning ahead, so you will generally find that VIPs are not crisis-prone.

Titled Guests

Titles are not a major problem in this country. Almost any casual encounter you will have with a titled person can be handled by "Ma'am" and "Sir." There are also reference books you can buy, such as the *Dictionary of Diplomatic Usage* and *Styles of Address*, which list all of the proper forms of address. You can always get a quick answer from any library that has a good reference department. Strange as it may sound, some large museums have protocol officers who have to know how to address and deal with foreign visitors. They can be a useful resource both for titles and questions about do's and don'ts. If all else fails, call the United Nations headquarters in New York.

Since ours is a democratic rather than a monarchic society, very little attention is given to proper forms of address. We happen to find it interesting to know that if for some reason the Archbishop of Canterbury checked into our hotel, we would address him as "Your Grace," while the Archbishop of New York would be "Your Excellency." We still cringe at the memory of bellmen shouting, "So long, Prince" to a member of Saudi Arabia's royal family. Princes are "Your Highness" the first time they are addressed; thereafter "Sir."

Should you be fortunate enough to be presented to the heir to the British throne, wait for him to speak *first*, and address him as "Your Royal Highness."

Summary

So who are guests? They are people. All kinds of people from all walks of life. They all want to be acknowledged as individuals and to be treated with respect. As we have discussed, they have many needs and desires. Your response to them can make the difference between a memorable event and just another trip.

TOPICS FOR REVIEW AND DISCUSSION

1. Discuss the importance of guests to hotels.

2. What are the differences among the six market groups?

3. Is the "Guest-History File" worth the effort?

4. Networking with other concierges can make a big difference to the level of service you can provide. Discuss the networking concept and how to use it.

5. Discuss some of the opportunities concierges have for educating their guests about the services they provide.

6. Discuss ways of coping with guests who aren't sure what they want

QUESTIONS

1. What are the six basic markets from which guests come?

2. What are some of the needs of convention attendees?

3. How does the concierge use the Arrivals report?

4. What is the advantage of a concierge network?

5. What is a "welcome note" and how do you use it?

6. What are the major types of requests a concierge must deal with on a daily basis?

7. What points should you remember when dealing with a guest's complaints?

8. Name three resources to use for researching your guests.

9. How would you research the proper forms of address for titled personages?

PROJECTS

1. Research the various ways of getting from a hotel in your town to some of the sightseeing attractions. Choose the best routes and practice giving precise directions to your "guests."

2. Interview the convention sales manager of a large hotel in order to learn what is involved in booking a convention.

CHAPTER 5

BASIC TRAINING/ ON-THE-JOB TRAINING

5

Official hotel training is primarily on-the-job training. As a new concierge you will usually be given a tour of the departments with which you will be most concerned (reservations, room service, and housekeeping), but this will not be an in-depth indoctrination. You should make an effort to return to these departments on your own to familiarize yourself with how they operate and how you, as a concierge, affect their operation. Be sure to get the names of the people you meet on your tour so that you have someone specific to go back to later for more in-depth information. This is also the beginning of your in-house networking system. Become aware of how your fellow employees affect your work in trying to fulfill guest requirements. Ask the Front Office Manager to show you various room types. Particularly if you are in a luxury property, knowing what room a guest is occupying will give you an immediate clue to both his taste and budget.

The one area in which you will be able to spend a reasonable amount of time is the study of the computer system. Knowledge of how the computer is used will be of great value to you, and you must take the initiative to see that you are properly trained in its use. Many hotels will make a terminal available to you, usually in the Reservations Department, where you may practice until you become proficient.

Since computer systems vary tremendously, we will not discuss actual computer mechanics. You will become familiar with your particular system by working with the other concierges on your staff. Depending on the size and organization of your hotel property, you will join the staff either at the concierge desk on the main floor or on the concierge level. If you are on the main floor, there will be the normal front desk operation to handle the check-in/check-out functions. If you are assigned to the concierge level, which is a less hectic place for training, you will have the additional responsibility of checking guests in and out, blocking rooms, and posting charges to their accounts. You will have covered this in your front desk unit, so we will briefly review the procedures in Chapter 12.

For now, we'll discuss two occasions when the concierge will use the computer system:

1. checking arrivals
2. leaving and deleting messages for guests

Once again, the exact mechanics of these processes vary depending on the hotel's property management system, so we will not go into this in detail.

1. *Checking arrivals.* Miss Almon's sister wants to have flowers sent to her, but she can't remember exactly when Miss Almon is due in town. A reservation search will give you this information. It's important to verify the arrival date when arranging for any kind of special amenity. Plans change, and reservations do get canceled. Remember never to give out a room number.

2. *Leaving messages.* You've made dinner reservations for Mr. Waterman and want to confirm the place and time. Typing this message onto the computer activates the message light on Mr. Waterman's phone. He then has the option of calling the operator for his messages or, in some cases, reading them directly off his TV screen.

Forms and How to Use Them

While concierges who work on the concierge level will make much more extensive use of the computer than their colleagues working at the main desk, the other services they perform for guests are the same. All concierges will use the following forms in the course of their work:

1. *Paid-out.* (See Figure 5.1.) These are forms for cash amounts, charged to the guest's bill and paid out (hence the name) by the cashier. Most properties require that the guest initial these forms. For example, Mr. Jeffers suddenly remembers it's his anniversary and wants you to send your messenger for Godiva chocolates for his wife. After calling the store to determine the exact cost including tax,

ROOM #	DATE	AMOUNT	

DEPARTMENT

DO NOT WRITE IN ABOVE SPACE

DATE   19

NAME

ROOM OR
ACCT. NO.

DATE	SYMBOL	AMOUNT

DO NOT WRITE IN THIS SPACE

EXPLANATION

FORM NO. FO-0489

PAID-OUT

SIGNATURE-CASHIER

SIGNATURE-MANAGER

Figure 5.1 Paid-out.

you fill out a paid-out and go to the cashier who gives you cash. You give the cash to your messenger, who goes out to pick up the chocolates. When the messenger returns, you send the chocolates up to Mrs. Jeffers and give the sales receipt to the cashier, who staples it to the paid-out.

2. *Miscellaneous charge.* (See Figure 5.2.) These are forms for items charged to the guest's bill, and then paid for by the hotel's accounts payable department. For example, if the hotel has an account with a florist, any time you order flowers for

Figure 5.2 Miscellaneous charge.

a guest you would process a miscellaneous charge to that account. The florist submits the bill to the hotel for payment. These are also used for FAXes and photocopies. If your hotel has an arrangement that its guests may use an off-site health club, the admission charge is posted as a miscellaneous charge.

3. *Room service orders.* If someone calls and wants to order a bottle of wine to be delivered to his Uncle Fred upon arrival, use this form. However, you will find that most room service departments prefer to deal directly with their customers. This avoids misunderstandings involving costly food items and is generally

NEW YORK **Marriott**
MARQUIS

It is our pleasure to confirm
the following reservation for you

_____

_____

_____

Sincerely

Concierge
New York Marriott Marquis

Figure 5.3 Confirmation card.

more efficient. It is also an opportunity for room service to generate additional sales during the conversation. While care must be taken not to annoy the customer by transferring his call, in the long run, it will strengthen your relationship with the room service department if you can transfer the call to them. A follow-up call to room service will assure you that the order was taken properly and remind them that you have their best interests at heart.

Confirmation Cards

Use confirmation cards (Figure 5.3) to advise guests of the actions you have taken on their behalf. These are their records of reservations, theater tickets, and so forth, and are a reminder to them of what has been scheduled.

Logbooks

There is a great deal of record keeping the concierge must do that cannot be kept in the computer. Your best friend and most exasperating enemy is paperwork. Records must be kept of everything you do on behalf of a guest; otherwise, it is impossible to function. All of the various kinds of reservations you make must be carefully logged—failure to do this leads to chaos at the desk. A guest may make a request of one concierge, then call back to modify it on a day that particular concierge is not on duty. The concierge's colleagues must consult the log to find out what action has already been taken. If they are not able to determine this, they will have an extremely unhappy guest on their hands. Although the exact design and number of individual logbooks varies from one property to another, one principle remains the same: if you do it, write it down. If you don't, it may cost you a lot of money.

General Logbook

If your property has relatively little concierge business, it may be possible to enter all of the miscellaneous reservations in one book. Large, bound "Daily Log" books are designed for this and can be purchased at the better stationery stores. All concierges should read the logbook at the beginning of their shifts. In order to enforce this practice, some operations require that concierges initial the logbook at the beginning of their shifts to signify that they have read the current material. Any messages the Chef Concierge wishes to leave for his or her staff (special meetings, etc.) will also be written here, and it will be your responsibility to be aware of them. All records will be kept in order strictly by date. The information required is:

- Date
- Name of guest
- Room number
- Company with whom reservation is made

❑ **Time**

This applies primarily to limo and radio car companies, restaurants, and baby-sitters. In each of these instances, it is crucial that the purveyors of services know at exactly what time they are to provide them. A limo arriving at the wrong time can cause a guest to miss the theater or, worse yet, an airplane. Restaurants will hold reservations only for a limited time after the hour specified for your guest's arrival.

❑ **Number of persons (if restaurant reservation or limo)**

It should be pretty obvious that a restaurant needs to know the table size and a limousine company needs to know whether to send a regular car or a stretch.

❑ **Name of company representative taking order**

No matter what anyone tells you, people make mistakes and foulups. Maitre d's promise you a table and forget to note it in their books. Limousine companies go to the airport on the wrong day. If you have a complaint, you must have the name of the person who took the order from you in order to substantiate that you know what you're talking about. It is also much easier to deal with the person you originally spoke to.

❑ **Name or initials of concierge**

If there is a problem with any reservations, it is important that you and your colleagues be able to identify whose work it is. This is not for purposes of placing the blame for something gone wrong, but for ease of correcting the situation. If you are keeping only one logbook that includes those types of reservations for which concierges are paid commissions, the initials of the person signing the order in the logbook will determine who gets the commission.

Limousines and Radio Cars

It may be easier for you to keep a separate log for these services. They will be used frequently for entries and referred to just as frequently when there are problems.

Record the following:

- ❑ Date of logbook entry
- ❑ Name of guest
- ❑ Room number
- ❑ Date car is needed
- ❑ Time car is needed
- ❑ Where pickup is to be made

  Pickups are frequently made at places other than the hotel. Drivers have to know the correct spelling of the guests' names so that they can make cards to hold up, and know the exact location where they are to meet their fares. When meeting someone at an airport, drivers need to know the flight number and city of origin.

- ❑ Length of time car is required
- ❑ Destination
- ❑ Credit card number
- ❑ Concierge's name or initials
- ❑ Name of limo company representative taking order

Restaurants

- ❑ Date
- ❑ Name of guest
- ❑ Room number

- ❑ Name of restaurant
- ❑ Number of guests
- ❑ Date of reservation
- ❑ Time of reservation
- ❑ Restaurant representative taking reservation
- ❑ Name or initials of concierge

Babysitters

- ❑ Name of guest
- ❑ Room number
- ❑ Number of children
- ❑ Sex and ages of children
- ❑ Date sitter is required
- ❑ Time sitter is required
- ❑ Approximate length of time sitter is required

Tickets

It is imperative that concierges who deal with a ticket agency keep accurate records of these orders. At the end of the month, the agency pays a commission based on the number of tickets sold, and you may need to substantiate your sales.

- ❑ Name of guest
- ❑ Home phone number (or room number if they are already in the hotel)
- ❑ Date tickets are required
- ❑ Time (evening or matinee)
- ❑ Number of tickets

- ❑ Preferred show
- ❑ Second choice
- ❑ Price range concierge is authorized to spend
- ❑ Credit card number
- ❑ Name of person at ticket agency taking the order

Tour Sales

Each tour company that you deal with will provide you with ticket books. Complete information is to be found in Chapter 6.

Phone Manner

We've all seen pictures of concierges holding a telephone to each ear and thought, "How contrived." Actually, it is not at all unusual for a concierge who is working the desk alone to be on two phones at once. When an airline puts you on hold, you can use this time to call a restaurant for a reservation.

Developing a pleasant telephone manner is crucial to a concierge. No matter how hectic things get, you must never give the impression that you are rushed. Answer the phone quickly and cheerfully, remembering to state your name: "Good morning, concierge George speaking," should suffice. Remember to smile; people can hear your smile over the phone.

Sometimes, of course, it will be necessary to put people on hold. This always annoys them. Do it as gracefully as possible. Ask, "Can you hold, please?" and wait for an answer rather than just saying, "Hold please," and slamming down the receiver. Some people will prefer to call back. Some people will leave a number and ask that you call *them*. And some people will say, "I can't hold, I'm calling long distance." Explain the situation that prevents you from speaking with them immediately: it could be that you are on another long distance call, you have four guests standing in front of you demanding your attention, or there is a crisis for you to resolve.

Most people will understand. Sometimes the guests at your desk will indicate that they are in no hurry and that you should take the call. But there are, alas, some people who just refuse to yield and will threaten to call the General Manager if you don't attend to them immediately.

One of the challenges of being a concierge is keeping a maximum number of people happy using a finite number of resources. (No matter how many phone lines are ringing, you can only talk to one person at a time.) The more hectic things get, the more charming you must become. While talking on the phone, maintain eye contact with waiting guests, smile at them, indicate that you're aware that they're waiting and that you'll be with them as soon as possible. Don't sacrifice efficiency and accuracy for speed. Waiting guests who have the opportunity to observe your manner in dealing with others will feel confident that you will give their requests the same careful attention.

Observing Before Acting

Be prepared to spend your first few days on the job observing. No hotel is going to throw you into the front lines without a chance to become familiar with the current operating systems and your new colleagues. You will find that you will just naturally start answering questions and providing information to the guests. Before you know it, you'll be on your own and will be able to confidently deal with guests. During this initial period, if you don't understand a procedure, ask for clarification right at that time when the example is fresh in your mind. This is the time when you should make yourself familiar with your property's systems, logbooks, equipment, supplies, and so forth.

TOPICS FOR REVIEW AND DISCUSSION

1. Discuss the importance of keeping logbooks. What are the various ones that may be required?

2. Discuss what constitutes a good telephone manner and why it is important.

QUESTIONS

1. What is on-the-job training?

2. Explain the difference between a paid-out and a miscellaneous charge.

3. What is a confirmation card? When would you use it?

CHAPTER 6

SERVICES PROVIDED
BY A CONCIERGE
(O U T - O F - H O U S E)

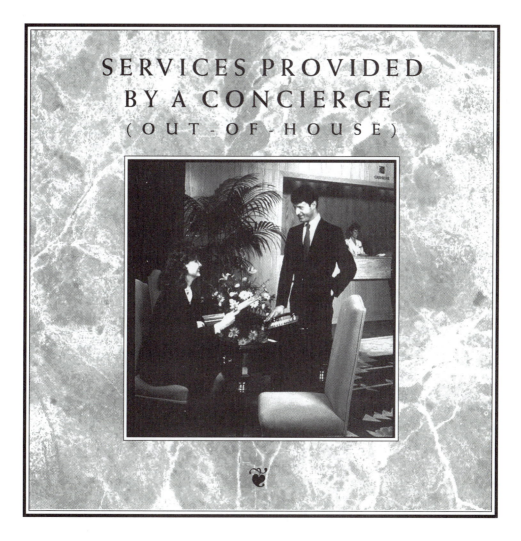

6

Although as a concierge you may be called upon for almost any service, the bulk of your work will fall into a limited number of categories. The following is a detailed explanation of those services and how to provide them.

Reservations

Airlines

It is essential to establish a working relationship with a nearby travel agency that will issue, deliver, and resticker tickets. Restickering is necessary when a guest already has a ticket but has changed flights. There is no change in destination or fare involved. Leave it to travel professionals to work out the details of connections, fares, and routing. They have their own highly sophisticated computers for this purpose. Be sure to ask guests ahead of time about routing or verify it with them immediately after getting the information from the travel agent. Long layovers are the bane of the frequent traveler's existence, and a guest will sometimes prefer to depart at a different time of day than was first indicated to you rather than be subjected to waiting several hours at an airport.

You *must* learn to read the OAG (*Official Airlines Guide*). North American and International editions are published monthly, and they are the Bible of the air travel industry. They're really quite simple, once you get the hang of them. Most people will merely want to know carriers and times.

The OAG is arranged by *destination;* under each city, it shows what flights *arrive* there. Therefore, if you want to know what flights leave from Phoenix to Atlanta, you start by looking under A for Atlanta. Go through the Atlanta listing until you find the origin city, Phoenix. All flights from Phoenix to Atlanta are arranged by departure time. The carrier codes are in the fourth column. Frequent use will acquaint you with most of these, but in your spare time, you will find it pays to study the abbreviations chart in the front. AA may be obvious, but does "Finnair" really spring to mind when you see the initials AY? The fifth column contains the flight number.

Some large cities have more than one airport; the various codes are located directly below the initial city listing. If you're working in New York, for example, you can efficiently inform your guests whether they'll be departing from La Guardia (L), Kennedy (J), or Newark (E).

The very first column tells you what days the flights occur. If it is blank, the flight departs daily. Following the code 1 = Monday, 2 = Tuesday, 3 = Wednesday, and so on, if the flight leaves only on Tuesday, there would be a 2 in that column. An X preceding the number indicates that the flight does not operate on that day. For example, X7 means that the flight departs daily except Sunday. The listing

3:05p ORD 5:33p DFW AA 389

indicates that American Airlines flight 389 departs daily from Chicago (O'Hare Airport) at 3:05 P.M. and arrives in Dallas–Fort Worth at 5:33 P.M.

Many guests will drop off their tickets when they request that you confirm a reservation. Guard these carefully and insist that the guest pick them up in person (most will want to). Never, never return tickets by sliding them under a door. Guests change rooms, bellmen misread numbers, and the results can be disastrous.

If a guest asks that you change a flight, be sure to have the ticket in hand before calling the airline. Deregulation has brought about such a wide range of fares, each with their own restrictions and penalties for change, that you will surely be asked the fare basis. If there is a penalty involved, be sure to verify that the guest is willing to pay the difference before authorizing any changes. Once the reservation has been changed, you will need to have a sticker put on the ticket with the correct information. Your travel agent will perform this service for you.

If you are purchasing a ticket for guests, they might either request that it be put on the room bill (not all properties allow this) or wish to pay for it separately by credit card. If they want it added to the bill, process a paid-out for the ticket amount and give the cash to the travel agent. Since the credit card companies take a percentage, some hotels add a service charge on all paid-outs over a certain amount—verify the exact procedure with your Front Office Manager or cashier. If your guest opts to use a credit card, make an imprint of the card on a Universal Credit Card Voucher (your travel agent will supply these), and have the guest sign it. The travel agency will fill in the amount later.

Babysitters

Every large city has bonded agencies that provide excellent babysitters on short notice. Unless you are setting up a new concierge desk, your property will probably have made arrangements with one of these already.

In most cases, parents will call you weeks (or months) in advance of their arrival to arrange for this service. However, it sometimes happens that someone will call for a sitter on very short notice.

You must ask parents:

1. Child's age and sex

2. Day, date, and hour the sitter is needed

3. Length of time they anticipate needing the sitter.
   (Are they planning just an evening out, or will they require someone all day?)

You must tell them:

1. The minimum number of hours; the hourly rate; carfare

2. Whether the hotel insists that the sitter be paid in cash or will allow you to do a paid-out against the guest's account

The purpose of asking the child's age is so that the agency can choose an appropriate sitter. They generally will send a young, energetic person to care for an active child and match an older, reassuringly motherly type with an infant. Parents with very young infants might wish to speak directly with the agency, and it's perfectly fine to give out its phone number. It's natural for them to be concerned

about leaving their child with a stranger in a strange hotel in a strange city. A sitter in Chicago once confided to us that the worried father had insisted on taking a Polaroid snapshot of her before departing for the evening—he wanted something to show to the police in case she kidnapped his child. (But this is an extreme case.) We have never had the slightest problem dealing with babysitting agencies. They have always been professional, dependable, and thoroughly reliable.

One word of warning: Do not call a friend or fellow employee if you're in a bind. The hotel could be liable for a major lawsuit should anything go wrong.

Hotels

You will frequently be asked to make a reservation for the next destination on your guest's journey. This request can range from, "Can you recommend a good hotel in Topeka?" to "Please book my usual two-bedroom suite at the Savoy for five days starting Thursday."

Guests will assume that you keep up to date on the newest and best hotels opening around the world (and well you should as part of your continuing self-education). But what if you don't know the best hotel in Topeka?

If your hotel is part of a chain, you will naturally start by consulting its Directory to see whether it has a property in the destination city. If you are not part of a chain, perhaps you are one of the "Preferred Hotels" or "Leading Hotels of the World." By sending your guests to another property in the same association, you assure them of similar quality. If your property has absolutely no affiliations, or if there is no space available, or if it doesn't meet the guests' requirements, consult the *Hotel and Travel Guide*. (See Chapter 8 for an explanation.) You can learn a lot just by looking at the pictures of the various hotels and comparing price ranges. Above all, never be afraid to admit that you are not knowledgeable enough to make a recommendation based on your own travel experience. Don't try to bluff. You really can't be expected to know everything. You must, however, have a method for researching and finding new information.

Once you have found the property, the procedure and information you need are the same whether you're booking Days Inn or the Ritz. You will need to know:

- ❑ Arrival day, date, and time
- ❑ Length of stay
- ❑ Type of room requested and approximate price range
- ❑ Credit card information to guarantee the reservation

If your guest will be a late arrival, a guaranteed reservation is an absolute necessity. Just a reminder, most hotels cancel nonguaranteed reservations at 6 P.M.—some even earlier. Even if your guests will be arriving considerably earlier, a guaranteed reservation guarantees them rooms in case of overbooking. Should the hotel be overbooked and not be able to provide your guests with a room that night, it is the hotel's responsibility to find them comparable rooms, provide transportation to the other hotel and back, pay for both the rooms and the transportation, and have rooms for them the following night. Savvy travelers always guarantee their reservations, and so should you. Be sure to inform your guests that they should call before the cut-off time for canceling guaranteed reservations if there are any changes in their plans, or they will be charged for the rooms whether or not they actually use them.

Depending on the length of advance notice and destination, you may telephone, telex, or send a FAX to the desired hotel for a reservation. The advantage of using either telex or FAX is that their response will be a written confirmation. If you make the reservation by phone, be sure to get a confirmation number and the name of that hotel's reservationist.

Enter this information into the appropriate log and write it out for your guests on a confirmation card.

By doing all of the above, you will have fully satisfied your guests' requests. But the enterprising concierge will go one step further, asking, "Will you need a limo to meet you at the airport in Topeka?" or "Are there any things I can arrange to have done for you in London?"

If the answer to either of these questions is "Yes," don't panic. Just call the concierge at the next hotel, who will be happy to provide this service for someone who will be his or her guest next, and you will have taken another step in establishing your network with other concierges.

When any of your VIP guests are traveling to a new location, call and alert the concierge to this. He or she will be on the lookout for your guests and will pamper them just as you would.

Limousines

Most hotels have a limousine company with which they work exclusively. The great advantage of this is that the limo charges can be added directly to the guest's bill as a miscellaneous charge, rather than a paid-out. Probably the most frequent requests are for airport pickups and theater calls, so we will discuss those first.

When guests call and request that a car be sent to bring them from the airport to the hotel, the following information is needed:

- ❑ Day, date, and time of arrival
- ❑ Airline and flight number
- ❑ Departure city
- ❑ Arrival airport (if your city has more than one)
- ❑ Credit card
- ❑ How many guests will be arriving and whether they have a great deal of luggage

The guests will probably ask you for the cost, so be prepared to tell them. Most limousine companies have a flat fee for airport pickups. Limousines are expensive, and at this point, they might well decide they'd rather take a taxi. If they decide to go ahead with the limo, relay all the above information to the limo company. They will call the airline to verify whether the flight is on time. The chauffeur will meet the guests at the baggage claim area and will be holding a small sign with the name of the passenger who made the reservation. Be sure to log all of this information.

Traveling to and from the theater by limo makes this event even more special. Most companies have a set price for the evening, which includes driving the guests from the hotel (or a restaurant) to the theater, waiting for them, then picking them up after the show and returning them to the hotel.

The minimum time for which a limo may be hired varies, but an hour-and-a-half minimum is pretty standard. What does this mean to your guests? Even if they just want a car to take them from the hotel to a business appointment across town, they will be charged for one-and-a-half-hours' use.

Even if your hotel has a company that it works with exclusively, you should have the names and phone numbers of several companies to use for backup. On rainy nights, it is not uncommon for all of a company's limos to be in use, and you will have to turn to other sources. Since these companies will not have an account with your hotel, inform your guests that they will have to pay by cash or credit card.

Radio Cars

An alternative to a limousine that we have used with great success is a radio car. The better companies use Lincoln Town Cars, or something equally spacious and comfortable. They normally do not have an hourly minimum and are therefore much more economical for short trips around town. Some guests, finding a limousine too flamboyant for their taste, prefer to use these smaller cars. They normally operate on a cash-only basis.

Make a point of getting to know the companies in your city and recommend the ones with the cleanest cars and most courteous and knowledgeable drivers. Some will be able to come to your rescue when you have a last-minute request for a private guided tour. If you are not able to engage a professional tour guide, explain your dilemma to the car company and request that they send someone who not only can drive, but can talk a little bit about the city. Guests are not necessarily interested in knowing the exact height of a building, nor the year in which it was built. They are quite content to have someone who can take them to the most interesting sights, wait for them while they take a few pictures, and return them safely. In a pinch, we have even used these car services to make urgent deliveries around town and to neighboring states. They are not cheap, but they are fast and reliable, and sometimes those are priceless considerations.

Railroads

AMTRAK requires reservations for its Metroliner service and for all Club (first class) seats. These are among the simplest reservations you will make. You need to determine:

- ❏ Day, date, and time
- ❏ Destination
- ❏ Number of people traveling
- ❏ Class of accommodation (first class or coach)
- ❏ Credit card information

Then call AMTRAK and make the reservation. You will be told the train number and exact departure time, and will receive a reservation number which your guests must use to pick up their tickets before boarding the train. These tickets can also be issued by your travel agency, which is the preferred method. Arriving at the train station with their luggage, your guests will usually be in a hurry and will not wish to stand on line for tickets.

Automobile Rentals

Should a guest wish to rent an automobile either in your city or from an agency in the next destination on his or her trip, you will need the following information:

- ❏ Day, date, and time the car is needed
- ❏ Number of days the car will be needed
- ❏ Whether it will be returned to the pickup location or will be a one-way drive (in which case the rental company usually adds a drop-off charge)
- ❏ Size of car (compact, midsize, full size)
- ❏ Company preference (Avis, Hertz, Budget)
- ❏ Any special account your guest might have with that company (Hertz #1 Club, etc.)
- ❏ Credit card

After speaking with the appropriate company and arranging for the rental, be sure to get a confirmation number from them. Ask for specific information on the rates and any mileage specials. Enter all of this information in the appropriate log book and send a confirmation card to the guest.

Recognizing that they get a great deal of business from concierges, some rental companies are actively seeking their business, offering preferential reservations and giving the concierges themselves special reduced rates. It's certainly worthwhile to have a sales representative from one of the companies attend a meeting of your local concierge society to explain how you can best work together.

Restaurants

"Where can we go for dinner?" is undoubtedly the most frequently asked question, and one of the most enjoyable to answer, for you get to be both a detective and a psychologist. One of the perks of working as a concierge is that you receive lots of invitations to restaurants; the owners realize that you are in a position to send them business and want you to recommend their place. Naturally, they know that you can do this a great deal more enthusiastically and sincerely if you've actually eaten there.

Guests will frequently ask you to describe the restaurant you recommend: What's the decor? Is it noisy or quiet? How are the people dressed? Are the tables very close together? Is this an appropriate place for a special celebration? Is it Nouvelle or Haute Cuisine? Anything on the menu for vegetarians?

Making a dinner reservation is more than just consulting a "City Guide" or "Where" magazine. All hotels provide some sort of directory or restaurant guide for their guests, but the guests value your opinion. Dining out is an expensive proposition these days, and people are not only looking for food but for an "experience"— particularly in a strange city. They are trusting their plans for the evening to you; they'll return home singing your praises and bragging about the "wonderful place" you sent them to if they're happy. If they are displeased, they'll be sure to let you know.

Do some legwork on your way to or from your hotel and get to know the restaurants in your neighborhood. Your budget may not permit dining in all of them, but you can meet the manager, ask for a sample menu, and get a feeling for the ambience. Then, when a guest asks you for a "romantic Italian restaurant within walking distance," you'll be prepared.

Let's start with a simple example: Mr. Harris calls and asks for a table for three at Da Umberto, tonight at 8 P.M. Can you call them immediately, or is there some more information you require of him?

You must ask whether he prefers the smoking or nonsmoking section. (To the despair of restaurateurs, nonsmoking sections must be provided.) You verify Mr. Harris's preference, and now you're ready to telephone Da Umberto.

Always introduce yourself by name, give the name of the hotel, and then state your request. Ask the name of the person who is taking the reservation. Here is a sample script:

CONCIERGE: Hello, this is Judy, the concierge at the Grand Hotel.
I'd like to make a dinner reservation for tonight, please.
A table for three at 8 P.M., in smoking.

RESTAURATEUR: Certainly, ma'am. What is the name, please?

C: Harris.

R: And the first name?
(You can use the computer to determine this if you haven't asked Mr. Harris.)

C: Richard.

R: Thank you. We'll see him tonight.

C: Thanks. And your name, please?

R: I'm Giuseppe, the Maitre d'.

C: Grazie, Giuseppe.

R: Con piacere, Signorina.

Now that the reservation has been made, two tasks remain:

1. *Log this information.* Mr. Harris may have gone out for a walk. He'll stop by the desk on his return and ask whether the reservation has been made. Either you or one of your colleagues will be able to verify this immediately by looking it up in the log. If, as can happen, Mr. Harris arrives at the restaurant and they have no trace of his reservation, you will have a record of the name of the person who took his reservation, and the restaurant will recognize their error and accommodate him.

2. *Send a confirmation note to Mr. Harris.* (See Figure 5.3) If your property doesn't have confirmation cards, a simple, handwritten note will do. In some larger hotels, you may leave the message for him on the computer. Include the following:

   - Name of restaurant
   - Address
   - Day and date
   - Number of guests and time

That was a very straightforward example. Unlike the decisive Mr. Harris, many guests won't have a specific restaurant in mind when they ask for your assistance. Some will just tell you they'll eat "anything good." In this case, it's often easier to start out by eliminating the cuisines the guests certainly don't want. However, most requests will fall into a few categories, and you can help guests speedily by having your information well organized. Guests will usually want to go someplace:

within walking distance	where the "tourists" don't go
romantic	near the theater
for Italian food	where there's music
for French food	for steak
for Chinese food	for brunch

When faced with an unusual request, such as Armenian food in New York City, it's best to admit that you don't know any Armenian restaurants off-hand but promise to research it and call the guest back. Try the Yellow Pages, or call another concierge. There is a great willingness to help one's colleagues in this profession, and we are all always learning, so don't be afraid to admit that you don't know something. If the guest's cuisine of choice simply doesn't exist in your city, suggest something similar.

Be aware of what the "in" places in your city are. Many popular restaurants accept reservations up to six weeks in advance and require reconfirmation the day before. It is vital that this be noted in your logbook. Imagine someone's displeasure if he has called you a month in advance to assure that he could celebrate his wedding anniversary at Le Cirque, then learns that they have canceled his reservation because it was not reconfirmed. He'll want your head on a platter.

On the other hand, it's also important to be aware of what places are riding on their reputations, have gone downhill, or about which guests have complained to you. We advocate gently steering guests away from them. This must be done both cautiously and tactfully, keeping in mind at all times that you don't know to whom you may be talking. For example, if a guest says, "I'd like you to book me a table for four at X," don't blurt out "Why on earth? The food there is terrible!" You might be addressing the Chef's sister. A polite "Have you been there recently?" or the ever-popular "Did a friend of yours suggest that you try X?" should alert the guest to the fact that it would not be on your list of recommended places.

The usual reply is, "I was there twenty years ago," or "Why? Don't you like it?" and you can continue from there, perhaps mentioning that some guests went there the previous week and complained to you about both the food and the service.

Concierges are sometimes placed in a difficult position by their own management when they are pressured to recommend in-house restaurants that do not measure up to their outside competition. There are several things to consider. First of all, if your restaurant is a good one, management should not have to pressure you. Part of your job is to support your own company, and your pride in having a good restaurant on the premises should lead automatically to its recommendation. You will also find that people know it by name and ask for it. Bad or indifferent restaurants are usually the fault of management. In this day and age, when culinary schools are training talented chefs, there is no reason for a restaurant not to hire a good one. For the same price one would pay to get an indifferent or poorly trained chef, one can hire a very good one. There are plenty to choose from, and their track records are no secret. Bad restaurants can usually be blamed on bad management: too much concentration on profit and too little on quality. It is very expensive to operate anything of quality, and restaurants are no exception. If you are blessed with the quality of management that spends the money to provide a superlative restaurant for its guests, by all means recommend it. But if your property has a restaurant that you cannot in good conscience recommend, follow your instincts. Don't recommend it. Nothing kills your reputation as fast as recommending bad restaurants. Because your reputation is a major factor in the success or failure of your hotel, it is in the best interests of the hotel to have you be honest about the quality of restaurants you send people to. Experience will soon teach you that unwarranted pressure from management is a sign that you should look for a better quality hotel. Keep in mind that guests normally do not choose to eat in the restaurants of their own hotels. They want to go out and see the other things the city has to offer.

It has unfortunately become a widespread practice for restaurants to "take care of" the people who send them business. By this we mean that many restaurants, usually of the middle ranks, will actually pay you so much per person to send them business. This is an ethical problem and, again, there are several things to evaluate and think about. The really good restaurants don't have to use gratuities as a substitute for quality. All restaurants are not equal, and you cannot allow yourself to make decisions based on your own income prospects. You must always make judgments based on quality. Sometimes other factors influence your final decision, but quality of service is your first interest. Restaurants that pay gratuities get a lot of business from concierges with low standards. But you will find that they can occasionally serve a purpose for you, too. They frequently have private rooms that are not available in the very best restaurants, and they are a good second line to fall back on when you can't get your guests into the restaurants of first choice. As one- or two-star restaurants, they are cheaper than their three-and four-star counterparts, and for many people this is the final consideration. They may also be closer to your hotel, and this is important in inclement weather. Always remember, the promise of receiving a few dollars for directing a guest to a lower quality establishment is not worth the trade-off of losing the guest's good will by a disappointing recommendation.

Tickets

Television Shows
Guests will frequently ask for tickets to the "Johnny Carson" or "David Letterman" shows. Tickets for most television shows of this quality must be ordered by mail, well in advance (up to a year and a half). There are, however, sometimes "same-day" tickets available. Call the TV stations to find out whether this is the case and to get

the details of how you should proceed in order to get tickets for your guests. Usually, guests will have to stand on line. Be aware that these details can change so it is important for you to call each time you need tickets.

Theater

For a concierge, ticket sales are as fraught with problems as restaurant reservations. There is a great deal of money involved in ticket sales, and they can be a major contributor, at no cost to the hotel, to the concierge's income. In a big city, the concierge can make thousands of dollars a month from commissions on ticket sales alone. This immediately puts ticket sales into that category of things that nobody wants to talk about. Somebody in the hotel is going to make a lot of money out of tickets unless the hotel management opts to use an outside company for this service.

Even if your property has an outside agency handling ticket sales, however, there will always be occasions (Sunday mornings and days when the agency personnel call in sick, for example) when you must procure tickets for guests. There are also those occasions when guests will tell you that the agency is sold out and they want you to find tickets . . . at any price. It is part of your mystique as a concierge that you can procure tickets to sold-out events, and guests will, of course, expect this of you. Proceed with extreme caution; the cost of tickets will be high. Dealing with "scalpers" can be hazardous to both your health and your job. It can also make you look wonderful if you establish solid contacts who really will get those impossible tickets for you. These people usually insist on being paid cash and are absolutely heartless about making exchanges. All sales are final. You cannot return the tickets, and if the guest won't pay for them *you* must or nobody will ever sell you another ticket. Here are a few tips for dealing with those occasions:

1. *Have your guests tell you an exact dollar amount of how much they are willing to spend.* "Money is no object," or "whatever it takes" are relative terms. We've had guests confidently ask for "Phantom of the Opera at any price," and then turn white when we quoted $250 per ticket.

2. *Get the money,* especially if someone is calling from out-of-town. You cannot realistically expect a stranger to lend you several hundred dollars, but that's exactly the position you'll be put in because you must pay for the tickets when they are delivered, which may be several days before the guest arrives. Suggest that the guest send a certified check or travelers' checks by Federal Express.

3. *Deal only with an agent you trust.*

For a detailed example, let's assume you are selling tickets for your hotel. Frequently, your guests will have no idea what they want to see, and part of your job is helping them decide. Are they in the mood for a musical or a dramatic play? Serious or comedy? Long-running success (*A Chorus Line*) or a show in preview? Broadway or off-Broadway? Perhaps they'd really prefer the ballet. It's vital that you know what's playing in your city, and a few minutes spent perusing the Arts section of the newspaper will pay off handsomely.

Most theaters now use a ticket service (Ticketron, Teletron, etc.) for phone orders. To place an order, you will need a major credit card and the following information:

- ❑ Name of play
- ❑ Day, date, and time of performance (evening or matinee)
- ❑ Number of tickets
- ❑ Location (orchestra, mezzanine, balcony)
- ❑ Credit card holder's name
- ❑ Card number and expiration date
- ❑ Issuing bank (for VISA and MasterCard)
- ❑ Billing address
- ❑ Daytime and evening phone numbers

If you do not have a computer to access all this information about your guests, we recommend asking them to write this out while you are dialing the ticket service.

The ticket service will inform you what price tickets are available for your requested performance. Although they will quote a general location (orchestra, rear mezzanine, etc.), they will *not* give you the exact seat numbers. These are computer selected. The company's service charge per ticket varies from $1.00 to $3.50.

Verify that the proposed tickets are acceptable to the guest, and be sure to include this sentence:

"This is a final sale—the tickets cannot be exchanged or refunded. Once I say, 'Yes,' they're sold. Shall I go ahead and place the order?"

If there is any hesitation on the guest's part, whether she's not sure because her husband is still out at a meeting, or cousin Hilda hasn't told them whether or not she'll be joining them, do not place the order. Tactfully suggest that after the guest has finalized her plans, you would be happy to call again. However, particularly if you are dealing with a very popular show, point out that tickets may not be available later. Let the guest decide.

If she wants to order the tickets at that time, give all the above information to the ticket service. Enter this information in your ticket sales logbook, then write out a confirmation card for the guest with:

- ❑ **Name and address of theater**
- ❑ **Day, date, and time of performance**
- ❑ **Number of tickets and location**

Advise the guest to be at the theater approximately one-half hour before curtain time to pick up her tickets. She will have to present the credit card in order to claim them.

Now it's time to get creative; show your concern that your guest's evening be a total success by asking, "Do you have any dinner plans yet?" or "Shall I order a limousine to take you to the theater and back?" She will appreciate this added effort on your part to assist her with her plans.

Sporting Events

Major stadiums use ticket services just as theaters do, and the same information is required when ordering tickets by phone with a major credit card. It is extremely helpful to have a stadium seating plan so that you can point out to your guests where they will be seated.

Tours

Selling tickets for sightseeing tours is another aspect of the concierge's job, and one that allows you to earn commissions. All major tour companies (Gray Line, Short Line, etc.) as well as your local companies will happily provide you with brochures and ticket books. Most will invite you to take a complimentary tour to become acquainted with their services. Have the brochures readily available, so that when guests inquire about such tours you can hand them the brochures quickly. The tours generally range from a two to three hour introductory overview of the city to all-day excursions including meals. The shorter tours are the most popular; people don't want to spend all day on a bus. Be sure to read the fine print—the hours of the tours vary seasonally. Whether or not you need to make reservations for the tours varies from city to city. Some companies anticipate business based on the previous years' volume; others require reservations. Know the policy in your city.

After the guest has determined the tour of choice and informed you how many adults and children will be participating, you calculate the total tour price. (Your sales representative from the tour company will have provided you with a rate schedule.) Carefully fill out the ticket, indicating the date, tour number, time, and number of persons. The deposit is paid to you in cash. The balance is to be paid directly to the tour company at the departure point—also in cash. The deposit is your commission.

We have known some concierges who consider it beneath their dignity to sell tour tickets, and we strongly disagree with this attitude. You are providing a service for your guests. A stranger in your city does not want to be told that he can "just pick up the tickets at the bus station." He is away from home, afraid of getting lost, and needs the security of a ticket in hand, showing that the following day at 10 A.M. he will be taking a tour of this unique and wonderful place.

Tour Guides

As an alternative to standard guided tours, many guests will ask that you hire a private guide for them. Perhaps English is not their native language, perhaps they hate buses, perhaps they just want exclusivity and have the means to pay for it. If you are working in a luxury property, chances are that qualified guides will periodically stop by to introduce themselves. If you are a newcomer to the profession, you can call your local convention and visitors' center for a recommendation, or you can use our preferred method: ask another concierge. Some guides have a minimum length of time (three hours is pretty standard) for which they will accept an engagement. Be sure to verify:

- ❑ Day, date, and time of the tour
- ❑ Price per hour
- ❑ Mode of transportation (walking tour, or rent a limo or radio car as well?)

Many guides will express their thanks to you by sharing a small percent of their fee.

Miscellaneous

How to Order Flowers

If the hotel has a flower shop on the premises, transfer this request to them, and they will handle everything, including charging the cost to the guest's room or credit card. If your hotel does not have a florist on the premises, you will have to use an outside source. Should your hotel have an account with a particular florist, the charge can be processed as a miscellaneous charge and posted to the guest's account. If this is not the case, you must get a credit card number when taking the order. Most vendors will not process credit card orders without all of the following information:

- ❏ Card number
- ❏ Expiration date
- ❏ Issuing bank (if MasterCard or Visa)
- ❏ Cardholder name
- ❏ Address
- ❏ Phone

Many large cities have twenty-four-hour florists. Find out who they are and enter their names in your Little Black Book. (See Chapter 7.)

Determine the following:

- ❏ To whom the flowers are being sent
- ❏ Date required
- ❏ How much the giver would care to spend
  (Tip—Keep track of the prices of roses as Valentine's Day approaches. They skyrocket.)
- ❏ The sort of floral arrangement the giver has in mind
- ❏ The message that should be on the card
  (It's easy to overlook this one.)

It may be the responsibility of the concierge to place flowers in a guestroom before the guest arrives. Caution must be exercised to be sure the guest will actually occupy that particular room. It's entirely possible that the front desk will change the guestroom without being aware that flowers have been delivered. Unfortunately, merely writing "Do Not Move" on the reservation card or typing it into the computer are not enough to prevent this from happening. While it is indeed lovely to throw open a door in a strange city and find a bouquet of flowers from your sweetheart, it's distressing to arrive home after the trip and discover that your flowers were delivered to someone else. Some guests will return missent flowers; others won't. And anyone can mistakenly assume that flowers with a note from "Your most ardent admirer" are for her.

Massages

When your shoulders are in a knot and your neck feels like a steel rod, there's nothing like a massage for total relaxation. Travelers are increasingly taking advantage of this luxury. Masseurs and masseuses with portable massage tables can set up shop in hotel rooms.

Be sure to use only licensed massage practitioners. When scheduling a massage for a guest, carefully note day, date, time, and name of the masseur or masseuse. It is customary for massage practitioners to give you a commission for choosing them.

Secretarial Services

Traveling businesspeople frequently need a report retyped, have letters to dictate, or a resumé to update. Many hotels now feature their own business centers. If this is not the case, there are two ways of dealing with this.

1. *If it's a small job, ask someone in-house.* Everyone can use some extra cash, and the General Manager's secretary or perhaps someone in Sales who has access to a typewriter can frequently assist you during their lunch hour or after work. Treat them professionally, pay them the going rate, and you've got a friend for life.

2. *Engage someone from a professional secretarial service.* It's possible to FAX work to these people and have the resulting documents delivered by messenger. Their rates can seem exorbitant ($50 per hour after 9:00 P.M. is not uncommon), but when you need some work done in a hurry, these people are worth their weight in gold!

TOPICS FOR REVIEW AND DISCUSSION

1. Discuss the importance of having a dependable travel agent.

2. Discuss the contents and uses of the *Hotel and Travel Index.*

3. Discuss the ethical questions involved in accepting gratuities from restaurants.

4. What are the things that a guest expects from a restaurant other than food?

5. Discuss the pros and cons of dealing with ticket sales.

QUESTIONS

1. What information do you need to arrange for a babysitter?

2. How do you make a hotel reservation in another city if you are unfamiliar with the hotels there?

3. What information do you need to arrange for a limousine to pick up a guest who is arriving at an airport?

4. When should you recommend your own hotel's restaurants?

5. What is the final thing you should always tell your guests about tickets they have purchased?

6. How do you get your commission on sales of tours?

7. If someone calls on the telephone and wants to order flowers to be placed in a guestroom, what do you do?

8. How do you arrange for secretarial services for a guest?

CHAPTER 7

SELF-EDUCATION/ CONTINUING EDUCATION

Athorough knowledge of your city is essential to both your success as a concierge and to your enjoyment of your work. Unfortunately, you will probably receive little training in this from your employer. It's strictly a matter of self-education. Although you will have maps and possibly city magazines to consult at your desk, the pressure of your work with the public will allow little time for research. When a guest is standing in front of you, he or she wants the answer *now* . . . and there is almost always a guest standing in front of you. Being a concierge has frequently been compared to being on stage, and you'd better know your lines before the curtain goes up!

Fortunately, the questions guests most frequently ask fall into several general categories depending on the day and shift you are working, and with a little homework you can be prepared to astonish them with your seemingly encyclopedic knowledge. For example, concierges working on Sunday mornings will invariably be asked for the Mass times at the closest (or most famous) Catholic churches; where to go for brunch; which stores will be open; when and how to get there.

First, we will cover some of the general ways to be prepared, and then we will get quite specific about how you organize your own book of information. The latter is of primary importance to you. Your "Little Black Book" of information is your key to success, and it needs to be thought out and prepared with care. Information gathering and self-education is an ongoing process and will continue for the lifetime of your career as a concierge.

Remember that as a concierge you will deal with practical considerations. Guests and hotel management come to you for help with real problems. You will be surprised at the outset to find that you really know very little about your city and the things it offers. Don't be dismayed when you don't have all the answers. Start with the most basic things. Learn the subway and bus routes from your hotel to the main sightseeing attractions (museums, tallest buildings, ballparks, etc.). In most cities, the transit authority will happily provide you with this information. The Hyatt

Regency in Chicago has gone so far as to have cards printed with directions by subway, bus, and car to major sights, a splendid idea that not only increases the concierge's productivity but insures that there is no confusion concerning the directions.

Guests who are coming to stay in your hotel will frequently telephone you from their homes to ask for directions to the hotel. Be prepared for this question. Write out the exact directions for driving to your property from the local airports and nearby cities. When the telephone rings, read the information to the guest and be sure that he writes it down. Remember that he is nervous about becoming lost en route and be patient when he asks you to repeat the directions several times. Be specific, as in the following example.

Directions to the New York Marriott Marquis from:

Northeast (Connecticut, Massachusetts, Rhode Island, etc.)

Follow the New England Thruway (I-95 South) to the Cross Bronx Expressway West. Follow signs to the Henry Hudson Parkway South. Stay in the left lane to enter the Parkway. Exit the Parkway at Fifty-sixth Street, turn left, and proceed east to Ninth Avenue. Make a right on Ninth Avenue (it's one-way) and head south to Forty-sixth Street. Turn left on Forty-sixth Street. The hotel entrance is on Forty-sixth between Eighth Avenue and Broadway.

Any telephone conversation with an arriving guest is a major opportunity for a good concierge. This is a chance to offer your services in providing for her needs while she is a guest in your hotel. Find out how many people are in her party. Why is she coming? Is this a business trip? Is she bringing her family? Are there young children? This is your chance to determine what specific needs she will have and to arrange to take care of those needs for her. This is the time to ask about restaurant reservations, babysitters, theater tickets, and all of the other things that she will want. This is when she learns about the many services you can provide to make her life easier and to improve the quality of her stay. It is also her first real contact with the hotel's personnel, and your response to her simple question about how to find the hotel can assure that she will become a satisfied repeat guest.

Please note that sometimes guests do not want to deal with what we have discussed above. They may be busy or in a bad mood. You must develop your telephone skills so that you know when it is appropriate to be extra helpful and when it is prudent to supply only the information requested. You will learn this by experience.

Familiarize yourself with the museums; know what special exhibits are planned and whether admission tickets must be ordered in advance. Contact the museum's Director of Public Relations and ask to be placed on their mailing list—they'll be delighted. You may occasionally need to arrange for groups to visit, and the Director of Public Relations can be a good contact. They are always willing to help with special problems or to direct you to the proper person within the museum who can. The larger museums may have a specific department catering to groups and to foreign visitors. Many museums rent out their premises for special occasions. This is usually expensive but can be the perfect solution to questions about where to hold a corporate function or a large meeting.

Know your own neighborhood. Allow some extra time on the way to or from work to explore the area around your hotel. Walk up one street and down the next, making notes as you go (a tape recorder is good for this purpose). Many of your guests will ask you for the closest shoe store, ice cream parlor, delicatessen, drugstore, newsstand, and restaurants of various kinds. These are the kinds of questions you need to be able to answer in a split second, so your legwork will pay off handsomely.

Creating Your Own "Black Book"

As you start accumulating information, you will soon find that you are inundated with paper. Magazine and newspaper articles, advertising brochures, and lots of notes on little scraps of paper will become a real organizational problem. The point is not to see how much information you can gather, but to gather useful information and to assemble it into a system designed for easy retrieval. Do this *before* you start your job.

1. Refer to the list of topics below and select the topics you think will most likely apply to your city.

2. Buy a loose-leaf binder and enough dividers to have one for each topic you have chosen. Be sure to have some extras.

3. Make a divider for each topic you have chosen.

4. Arrange the topics (dividers) alphabetically in your book.

You now have the bare bones of your most basic and important tool—your own "Little Black Book." The following list of topics is provided to guide you and to help you develop your book more easily and quickly. They are a compendium of subjects we have found useful in *The Concierge's Guides*, a series of guidebooks based on our own Little Black Books. You will find that some of these headings will not apply to the cities in which you may work. Conversely, your city will almost certainly require headings not listed here. You must adapt your book to fit your own needs and the needs of the guests you serve.

As a novice, the best idea is to try to have a basic amount of information for each category prior to actually starting your job and to add to and eliminate as you go along. If you are assigned to a city of any size at all, you will find guidebooks evaluating everything from hotels and restaurants to the many out-of-the-way places that guests will never ask you for. Most of these books are poorly designed for information retrieval and will be useless to you on the job. They will be of use, however, as guides to which data to include in your Black Book. The Yellow Pages of the telephone directory is another wonderful source of basic information, particularly if you are establishing a concierge department. Also check all of the local newspapers and any magazines that might contain information about your city or area. You will find that all of these reference materials are good sources for names, addresses, times, and other basic data. You will also find that there are a lot of discrepancies in this information. You must personally check the accuracy of every entry you make to your book. You must also personally critique each and every place or service that is of real importance to you. We say "of real importance" because it is impossible to visit each place, eat in every restaurant, and examine every service you will recommend. All concierges have this problem. To compensate, you will share information with your fellow concierges, ask guests about their experiences, and read constantly about all of the things that affect your job and your hotel.

One of the most important pieces of information you will add to your book is the name of your contact at each place. Your guests are special, and you need to be able to call someone who knows you and the quality of service you require for your guests. This person must be prepared to make a special effort on your behalf. Nothing is more effective than a personal visit to the various places people ask you about. Dine in the restaurants; inspect the limousines; take the sightseeing tours; visit the stores and newspaper stands. Take notes to add to your Black Book. Keep them brief and to the point. Always eliminate anything that doesn't help you do your job and any data that are out of date. Data become obsolete very fast. Because you have gathered your information by subject heading, you will be able to glance down your list and see all of the entries you would recommend. You will be in a position to quickly make alternative suggestions when a guest is trying to make up his or her mind about what to do and see.

Using the topic you have selected, start by making a list of questions you would ask about these places if you were a tourist. Be sure to include in the following order:

- ❏ Name of entry
- ❏ Telephone number
- ❏ Complete address (include cross streets)
- ❏ Your contact's name (may be several)
- ❏ Hours of operation (days closed)

❑ Cost

❑ Credit cards accepted

❑ Your personal notes on quality, etc.

Arrange your information in a consistent format so that you know where to look for data quickly. Phone numbers are used more often than addresses, so put them first. Guests don't want to wait while you browse through a long list of information. Our personal Black Books have been published as a series covering the major cities of the United States. You may want to refer to one of *The Concierge's Guides* to see the type of layout that has proved to be most efficient for our use and for that of the many concierges in those cities. While you won't be able to create such a book without the use of a computer system for alphabetization purposes, your basic subject-heading breakdown will work very well for your purposes. Remember that when you are working by subject headings you must know the contents of your book well enough to know what subject heading contains what information. The process of actually compiling your own book will ensure that you have this knowledge. Creating a Black Book is not only an enormous challenge, it's a lot of fun. The following sections outline some of the possible subject headings that you may want to include in your own Black Book.

■ **AEROBICS CLASSES**

Due to the new trend toward physical fitness, more and more people are working out. When they travel, they want to continue with the same types of exercise they do at home. While many hotels and resorts now have their own facilities, it is rare to find in-house aerobics classes. You may need to find places that will take your guests on a one-time basis. Since most health clubs are based on memberships, it will be necessary for you to call all of the quality places to see whether they will accommodate your guests. It may be possible for your hotel to have an arrangement with a nearby club that will allow guests to use their facilities for a small fee. The best place to find a complete list of aerobics classes is the Yellow Pages of the telephone book. Call each facility and ask if they will take your guests on a one-time basis. If they say "yes," make an appointment and go visit them. If you like their operation, add all of the pertinent information to your book. When you call them to make reservations for your guests, be sure they understand that this business is coming from your hotel. The more they realize that you can send them business, the better care your guests will receive. Note that you have now created a new selling point for the hotel. It is important that you let the appropriate hotel personnel know so they can incorporate it into their marketing plans. Send a memo to your immediate superior with copies to everyone who might be affected. This might include the General Manager, Resident Manager, Marketing Director, Director of Sales, Public Relations Manager, Rooms Division Manager, Reservations Manager, and the Front Desk Manager. Since these people now know that this service is available through the concierge, they are able to market this service and to send additional guests to you. This is one way you create new business and repeat business for your hotel.

■ AIRLINES

Any hotel that can support a concierge has a clientele that depends on airlines for transportation. Using the Yellow Pages, make a complete alphabetical list of all of them. Include the various phone numbers they list for sales offices, lost luggage, executive offices, and, if possible, a number for international flights. Over a period of time you can eliminate the ones that are never asked for. The airlines business has a history of being very quixotic. Major airlines may merge with other carriers, changing their names and telephone numbers overnight. You must keep abreast of this. Aside from reading the business section of all of your newspapers (a must for a good concierge), you will want to periodically call the numbers on your list to be sure they are still accurate.

■ AIRLINE SHUTTLES

Your city may be served by "shuttle service" to nearby cities. If so, this is invaluable information to have at your fingertips . . . you will be asked for it constantly. Be sure to include schedules in your book as well as information as to whether one pays on the plane or has to purchase a ticket in advance. You will need to know exactly where the check-in counter is located. Since they can't always compete financially for prime space, shuttles can be located in obscure terminal buildings, and you need to know where they are and how to get there. Is there parking nearby and what does it cost? How long can you leave your car there? Again, be warned that shuttle information and schedules change constantly. You will have to keep up with it and keep your book up to date.

■ AIRPLANE CHARTER SERVICES

You will rarely be asked to charter a private plane, but when you are asked your guest is usually a real VIP. You need to know not only the names of the very best charter companies but exactly where they are. What airports do they normally use and what airports are they authorized to use? The fact that their offices are at one airport does not necessarily mean that they can't fly into another airport to pick up your guests. Frequently their offices will be quite some distance from your city. When you are chartering, you may be meeting some specific needs of your guests. For example, they may need a plane with special hospital facilities for transporting a sick or injured person. This service is available from many of the major companies. When required, you should be prepared to tell them the nature of the illness so they can be sure that they have proper equipment on board. These are unique circumstances, and you should not be shy about asking the charter company for help. Tell them what you have been asked to do and ask them what information they need in order to provide the best service. They tend to be extremely cooperative. This is another area where companies come and go. Stick with the major companies that have a track record of safety and performance. Be sure to find out what types of payment they accept.

You may need their services with no advance notice in the middle of the night when banks are not open. We have been able to use the American Express Gold and Platinum cards for some emergency charters.

■ AIRPORTS

This information is vital. Be sure you have exact information as to the location and how to get there. Most airports of any size can supply you with pamphlets providing all of the information about the services available, including phone numbers for airlines counters and airport services such as parking, security, foreign currency exchanges, shops, including those that are duty free, and automobile rental agencies. Call public relations and tell them who you are, the hotel you represent, and ask them to send you complete information about the airport. You will be amazed at what you find out about your airport.

Information on transportation to and from the airport will be needed constantly. The easiest way to break the data into usable segments is by type of transportation. It's a good idea to have distance information and travel times based on differing traffic conditions.

Driving. You will need exact directions for driving to and from the airport. You may want to include at this point information about the parking lots' availability.

Buses. List the names of the companies providing buses or the bus numbers (if they are city buses). Include the exact addresses of nearby bus stops and scheduled pickup times. If service is curtailed at night or on holidays be sure you know about it. What is the cost? Can they handle luggage? Where do they let passengers out at the airport?

Shuttle Buses. Most hotels are served by some type of shuttle bus that has regularly scheduled pickup times at the hotel. Tickets are either purchased ahead of time at the hotel (possibly from the concierge), or payment is made in cash to the driver. In either case, you may be required to call the shuttle bus company

SELF-EDUCATION/CONTINUING EDUCATION

to make reservations for your guests. Be sure you confirm these reservations to your guests and tell them exactly where the bus will pick them up. Guests are normally very concerned about the pickup location, and you do not want to be responsible for their missing their flight.

Taxis. Most people take taxis to and from airports. Be sure you know the approximate fares and the amount of time the trip will take under normal traffic conditions. Limousines and radio cars should not be included under this subject heading but should be listed under limousines and radio cars. (Note that radio cars are normally cheaper than limos and provide the same basic level of luxury.)

■ AMUSEMENT PARKS

Amusement parks abound on the American landscape. If there are any near you, it would be wise to list them until you can determine whether your guests ask you about them. If you have no requests for them, eliminate the data. If you are near Disneyland, Disney World, or any of the major parks you will certainly need this subject heading. List all of the usual data: name, phone numbers, address, hours of operation, and directions as to how to get there. It also pays to have a stock of their brochures to use as handouts. If you call their public relations department, they will certainly invite you to visit the park and become acquainted with what they have to offer your guests.

■ ANNUAL EVENTS

This is not silly information designed to fill up your book. Although you may never be asked about the St. Patrick's Day parade or a specific street fair, you will need to know that when they occur certain parts of the city are closed to traffic. That affects the amount of time it takes to get to and from the airports. It affects the cost of getting to the airports. It means guests should walk instead of taking taxis if they want to go into the affected areas. In addition to these practical considerations, knowing what events are taking place on any given day aids you in guiding tourists who ask for your advice about what to do with their time and how to enjoy the things that are unique to your city. Little extra insights on the events can be very useful to guests and spice up their visit. For example, in New York everyone goes to the Macy's Thanksgiving Day Parade. But most people don't know how much fun it is to go to the start of the parade route the night before and watch the balloons depicting Snoopy and his friends being inflated. You should know that it takes all night and that many people take blankets (it's cold) and picnic baskets.

■ ANTIQUES

You will frequently be asked questions about where the antique shops are. Since they tend to flock together, a general location is usually most helpful. The popular ones may be listed separately with their specialties. There is frequently a magazine or publication you might find useful as a handout. List the bus and subway stops closest to the shops and be aware that in the antique business, some stores deal only "with the trade" and are not available to the casual browser.

■ AQUARIUMS

If you work in one of the lucky cities with an aquarium, you have a major sightseeing attraction. Call the public relations department and have them put you on the mailing list so that you can keep up with special events. Ask if you can tour the premises. Arrange for them to supply you with their advertising brochures to use as handouts for your guests. Record all of the basic data in your book for quick reference. Don't forget hours of operation, when they are closed, and how to get there by public transportation.

■ ART GALLERIES

Like antique shops, galleries tend to cluster in specific sections of a city and can be listed by area in general terms. Many people are not buying art, they just want to browse and to visit areas where the action is and to see all of the shops and restaurants that spring up in the neighborhood. You may find it useful to list the buildings housing several galleries rather than the galleries themselves. A real buyer will ask you for the address of a specific gallery. The larger cities have publications called "Gallery Guides" that list everything you need to know. They are published monthly and list all of the galleries and their current exhibitions. The publisher will provide these for you to use as handouts.

■ **AUCTIONS**

Auctions are of interest to a very limited clientele. Fortunately, the few companies in this business tend to be very solid and stay in one place. It is worthwhile to list the major companies and their basic information.

■ **AUDIO VISUAL EQUIPMENT (See RENTALS, AUDIO VISUAL)**

■ **AUTOMOBILES (See RENTALS, AUTOMOBILES)**

■ **BABYSITTERS**

This is an essential service, and one much in demand. Try to see that your property has a close relationship with the very best agency. Guests are very concerned about leaving their children in a hotel with someone they don't know. Be sure that guests understand the charges. While basic charges are by the hour there can also be extra expenses. For example, if there is more than one child there will probably be additional charges per child; if the babysitter is kept after a certain hour there may be a carfare requirement; and there is always a minimum charge.

WARNING: This is one of the areas of service where you must exercise caution. Should anything happen to a child for whom you, as a representative of the hotel, have provided a babysitter, the hotel might be liable. You should never use an agency that has not been approved by your management. They should be sure the agency is reliable and bonded. Never use friends or fellow employees without management approval. This is not meant to frighten you, but as a concierge you represent your hotel and its management. You must be aware of potentially problematic situations and know how to handle them properly.

■ BALLOON RIDES

Balloon rides seem to maintain a certain level of popularity, and you may find it worthwhile to keep track of any in your immediate vicinity. Basic information and any points of real interest should be recorded. If you have no real call for this data, eliminate it.

■ BALLOONS

The balloon business has mushroomed in recent years. There are now all kinds of balloons for every occasion. The people who deliver them are frequently dressed as clowns, gorillas, or in formal wear. Some people like to have balloons delivered in addition to or as an alternative to flowers. We remember the looks of delight on the faces of guests in a major New York hotel when someone lost his hold on balloons filled with helium. They drifted slowly to the ceiling towing a large box of chocolate truffles. It required the combined efforts of the security and maintenance departments using a hydraulic lift to retrieve them.

■ BALLROOM DANCING (See DANCING)

■ BANKS (See MONEY MACHINES)

■ BARS (See also GAY BARS, PIANO BARS, SINGLES BARS, SPORTS BARS)

Unless you have famous bars in your town you will probably have no need for this category. Enter only the most basic data unless you want to make a personal note regarding food quality, music, or the reason for its fame.

■ BASEBALL

You might have a surprisingly large number of people ask you questions relating to sporting events. For baseball, you need the name of the team, where they play, how to get there and back, the telephone number for the box office (remember that other ticket outlets sell tickets for sporting events), and the season's schedule with starting times. Remember that traffic around a stadium is usually very heavy. Anyone driving to a game should allow plenty of time.

■ BASKETBALL

See considerations under BASEBALL.

■ BEACHES

If you are in a resort area you will receive lots of requests for information about beaches. You should seek out all of the basic data and add such things as: is there a lifeguard on duty? When? Is there food available? Are there bathrooms? Is there public transportation? Be sure you know what type of crowd frequents each beach.

■ BEAUTY SALONS

List only the very best. Guests are normally not interested in a bargain beauty salon. It will be of great value to you to get to know the owner or manager of the most important salons. They are normally busy, and you need a connection in order to assure your guests of prompt attention. If you have a salon in your hotel, make an effort to find out all about the services they offer and their pricing. It is always important to try to promote the businesses within your own property. Their success reflects on your hotel. They not only bring business into the hotel, they also pay a substantial rent. Anything that makes your hotel look good improves your position as a concierge. Find out what salons open early, stay open late, and are open on Sunday.

■ BICYCLES (See RENTALS, BICYCLES)

■ **BICYCLE TRAILS**

Maps showing the trails are usually available from city parks departments. These indicate the length of the trails and any special places of interest (such as restaurants or bathroom facilities) en route. Because of the complexity of the trails, the main information you can provide to a guest is where they start and end. Be sure to advise your guests concerning safety or personal security considerations.

■ **BOAT RENTALS (See RENTALS, BOATS, or MARINAS, or YACHTS)**

■ **BOOKSTORES**

Bookstores are an integral part of city life. Guests will usually ask for the nearest one. In addition to listing information about these, also include the biggest ones, stores that have a particular specialty (cookbooks or travel books, for example), and any that might be open late or on Sundays.

■ **BOW TIES (How to tie them)**

Knowing how to tie a bow tie will get you many tips. When someone is going to a formal dinner and can't tie his tie, he has a real problem. If you can't tie one, call room service or the Banquets Manager. All of their public contact staff wear bow ties. They are also a source for buying or borrowing a tie when all else fails. Tie departments frequently have available free of charge instructions for tying bow ties. Pick up a copy and keep it for easy reference.

■ **BREWERIES**

Breweries could fall under several other categories such as tours, restaurants, or sightseeing. Thus it is obviously easier to list them separately. This does not mean that you can't duplicate your information under any or all of the other subject headings. For this type of entry your personal critique is of great value. Be sure to visit the breweries to see if they are the sort of thing guests would enjoy as "a little out-of-the-way find." If so, include them in your book. Add all of the usual basic information. In your critique be sure to include the names of contacts you can call to arrange special attention for guests.

■ BRIDGES

When you are asked where a certain bridge is located, it is a big help to know which streets connect with it. It is a simple thing that can be of real use to you.

■ BUS LINES

List only special bus lines. Keep a stock of city bus maps.

■ CARS (See RENTALS, AUTOMOBILES)

■ CAVIAR

In major cities like New York and Chicago, caviar is a frequently asked-for luxury, and it is handy to know where it can be purchased. Some of the establishments selling in quantity also have restaurants that provide fine dining and feature caviar. Learn to discuss the varieties of caviar, the costs, and its proper service.

■ CEMETERIES

You may be surprised to find that cemeteries are frequently major sightseeing attractions. The burial sites of the famous are of great interest to many people. Cities like Boston, Washington, D.C., and Los Angeles treat them like any other attraction and often provide maps showing just who is buried where. If your hotel is near such a site, you will find it useful to have all of the basic data available. List the name of the cemetery, phone number (this might be the church or parish house administering the cemetery), and the address. The latter may be difficult to ascertain since so much ground is involved. You need to identify the main entrance that visitors should use. This can be done by listing the street the entrance is on and the cross streets. Hours of admission are important. They are normally open every day.

■ **CHILDREN'S ACTIVITIES**

This can be a huge listing, but you will find that you will use very few of them. Parents staying in your hotel are not looking for someplace to send their children while they do something else. What they want is something they can all do together that the children will find of real interest. There are several ways to collect this information. Look through the local magazines for lists of children's activities. All cities of any size have such magazines. Sunday editions of newspapers also carry this data in their travel sections. Duplicate any entries under SIGHTSEEING that seem suitable.

■ **CHINATOWN**

Chinatown, Japantown, and some of the other ethnic communities are of great interest as sightseeing attractions. They are also home to some of the most popular restaurants. The restaurants should be treated under that subject heading, and it is best to deal with Chinatown as an entity. People want to see the whole thing. Be sure you have a good idea of the streets that border the area and list several different methods of transportation. Include the bus and subway stops that are closest to the main activities.

■ **CHOCOLATE**

It is essential to have a list of the very best places to buy chocolate. No matter how expensive it is, guests want it. Many hotels have branches of famous name shops. Notice that the key word here is *best*. Don't bother with the rest. You will need the usual basic information plus a few comments about each shop's specialty... like chocolate truffles or strawberries hand-dipped in chocolate.

■ **CHURCHES**

Churches should be listed by denomination because guests will normally ask you for the "nearest Catholic church" or the "nearest Methodist church," etc. They might ask for one that is particularly well known. But experience will teach you which places are never asked for, and you will then have the option of eliminating them from your records. However, keep in mind when eliminating information or entries that as a concierge you are expected to have all information at your fingertips. Each time you eliminate data you run the risk of not having it available the one time you actually need it. A good practice is to eliminate only when space becomes a real problem or when one of your entries goes out of business.

■ **CHURCHES, HISTORIC**

Depending upon your city, this can be a really useful list. In Boston, there are many churches rooted in the history of our country and guests frequently want to visit them. The missions in California are also very popular, and Washington, D.C. has many churches where presidents have worshipped. Keep these in strict alphabetical order by church name. For your own ease of retrieval add one-line references to tell you who worshipped there or why it is important. For example, people will ask you where Paul Revere went to church. Add a single line that says: Paul Revere— see Old North Church. Keep all of your data under Old North Church. Do this for everyone whose church is asked for. One basic pool of data listed by church name can be referred to by many one-line entries by worshipper.

■ **CLOTHING**

We suggest that you subdivide this category (and cross-reference each) as follows:

Children's
Men's
Men's—Discount
Men's—Formal Wear
Men's—Shoes
Women's—Designers and Boutiques
Women's—Discount
Women's—Shoes

■ **CLUBS, PRIVATE**

Private clubs are not asked for frequently, but if they are it is usually a guest of importance who needs the information. A concierge who has this readily available will be considered "special" since private clubs are elitist by nature and keep a low profile. This data almost never changes so there is virtually no maintenance. Check the telephone numbers occasionally.

■ **COFFEE HOUSES**

Coffee houses come and go in terms of popularity. They tend to evolve in close proximity to one another and are frequently found near schools and universities. The information changes frequently, particularly their hours of operation, and must be watched carefully if it is to remain useful. Many of them boast some sort of music or entertainment, and that also changes constantly. Record all of the basic information and add some very short notes about entertainment. You may find it useful and perhaps easier to cut clippings from magazines and newspapers and insert them in your book at this subject heading. These can be changed as the coffee house changes its entertainment. Don't let this get out of hand. Nothing looks worse than a book full of scraps of paper that will invariably fall out when your General Manager is watching. (Better still, insert your clippings into plastic sleeves.)

■ **COFFEE/TEA**

Many people like to purchase freshly ground coffee and packages of tea when they travel even though they might never do so at home. Have available the names of some of the best shops and try to pay them a visit. They generally sell all kinds of paraphernalia connected with the brewing and serving of these beverages and can be sources for hard-to-find items. Include basic data plus a few notes. Watch their hours because they may change seasonally.

■ **COLLEGES/UNIVERSITIES**

Use a completely alphabetical list. Addresses are complicated because you are deal-ing with entire campuses. It is best to restrict yourself to the main address for most entries. If you are dealing with major institutions, however, there may be many indi-vidual buildings or separate schools within a university that you will find it useful to list. All you need for your record is name, address, and telephone numbers.

■ **COMEDY CLUBS**

Record all of the basic data as usual, then add some notes as to the general type of performer one can see there. Since this is data you will use frequently, you must keep up with their schedule. Again, this is a subject that changes on a weekly basis; it is hard to keep up with and you will have to be creative in order to do so. If you decide to clip schedules from magazines and newspapers, insert the COMEDY CLUB pages into plastic sleeves. Use a separate sleeve for each club and insert the clipped schedule next to your basic information.

■ **COMPUTERS (See RENTALS, COMPUTERS)**

■ **CONCERT HALLS**

Guests will require only the basic information. Be sure of addresses, phone numbers for box offices, and all of the bus and subway stops. This category is easy to maintain but must be accurate. A wrong address can cause a guest to miss a performance.

■ **CONSULATES**

Seldom requested, this information is invaluable when you are facing a VIP guest. Get your data right the first time and check phone numbers occasionally. The facts seldom change. Remember that all embassies are located in Washington, D.C.

■ **CONVENTION CENTERS**

The more you know about convention centers the better off you will be. Hotels service millions of people who attend conventions. Your data must include all of the transportation to and from the center, its hours of operation, notes about restaurants in its vicinity (including the ones with private rooms for groups) and any additional data that people frequently ask for. You should also be familiar with where the shuttle or special charter buses stop at your hotel to pick up your guests who are going to the center.

■ **COSTUME RENTALS (See RENTALS, COSTUMES)**

■ **CRUISE LINES**

This might not be a subject heading of importance to you. Guests will not normally ask a concierge to make arrangements for a cruise. On the other hand, you may have guests who want to know how to get to a particular ship or how to make a telephone call to a ship on the high seas. At that point it is helpful to have basic information about the cruise line. If you don't use this data over a period of time, eliminate it.

■ **CURRENCY EXCHANGES (See FOREIGN CURRENCY EXCHANGE)**

■ **CUSTOMS, U.S.**

For guests who travel internationally this can be useful. Keep only the most basic information, such as telephone numbers, because each guest will have a different problem requiring some research on your part. You may find it helpful to have a copy of current basic regulations that might affect your guests.

■ **DANCING**

Dancing is a difficult topic to keep abreast of because of the fluctuations in the popularity of any given place. What is "in" today is "out" tomorrow. That is one of the aspects of its popularity. Many people love the "trendy" and want to go to the latest clubs. Few of these take any sort of reservation and frequently admit people based on their looks rather than on a first-come, first-served basis. A more stable situation will be encountered in your pursuit of ballroom dancing. Restaurants are frequently the best (or only) locations featuring this type of entertainment. One will be required to have dinner, or, depending on the hour, drinks. The music is almost always provided by a live band and reservations are required. There is usually a dress code, and the clientele tends to be older than the club crowd. Your book should contain all of the basic information including the dress code. Add to that all admission and cover charges and any other data affecting the total cost to your guests (such as a two-drink minimum). Some establishments have unsavory reputations. Make it your business to know this so that you can steer your guests toward the better places. Anytime a guest has an unpleasant experience, it will color his or her memory of staying in your city and hotel.

■ DELIS

Delis should be listed under RESTAURANTS. Experience shows, however, that people know when they specifically want a deli, especially a Kosher one. They will probably ask for it by name. You may find it easier for quick reference to keep the few really good ones listed under both categories. There is usually one that is much better than its rivals, and you should be aware of this. Some of them will deliver food to your hotel. Also, a guest's decision will frequently be based on which one is closest to your hotel.

■ DELIVERY SERVICES

"Delivery service" is the proper term for long distance; messenger services are for local deliveries. Keep a list of the major delivery services (Federal Express, DHL, United Parcel Service, etc.) and the hours that they will pick up at your hotel, particularly the last pickup of the day. Be sure you have information on their rates as well as any size and weight restrictions for packages. The delivery service will probably ask you for the latter information as well as the address and Zip Code to deliver to when you call to arrange for a pickup. Be sure to know or you'll have to make a second phone call.

■ **DEPARTMENT STORES**

Locations and hours are essential—especially late and Sunday hours. Telephone contact with a department store is very difficult, so be sure to keep all of your information current. Hours are usually included in their newspaper advertisements. Find out which stores, if any, have Personal Shoppers . . . assistants who will either shop for your guests or will take them around the store personally to facilitate their shopping. An appointment will be required, but it can sometimes be arranged on very short notice. Some of the major stores now have their own "concierge" services, and it may be worth your while to contact them to find out what they can do for your guests.

■ **DISCOS (See DANCING)**

■ **DISCOUNT SHOPPING**

Depending on the quality of guest your hotel attracts, you might be asked for discount shopping or bargain stores. All you will need is basic information plus some idea of what each store handles. They are frequently open on Sunday and holidays and may be grouped together in one area of town.

■ **DOLLS**

While DOLLS also belongs under TOYS, there are peculiar requirements that make it worthwhile to list it separately. Dolls are not just toys, they are also collector's items and are sometimes of great value. The people who collect them are frequently interested in constructing, repairing, or decorating doll houses. All of this is highly specialized and can be quite expensive. Know which stores are the best, particularly in terms of repairs. Some shops of this type also include museums featuring antique dolls and houses, so you may want to include them under MUSEUMS as well.

■ **DOWNTOWN**

Know the general area comprised by this term and all of the bus and subway transportation serving it.

■ **DRUGSTORES/PHARMACIES**

List the nearest and any that have late and Sunday hours. Be sure you know whether they will deliver to your hotel and whether there is a registered pharmacist on duty at all hours.

■ **DRY CLEANING/LAUNDRY**

List basic information about the ones that can provide service when your hotel can't, the ones that have extra fast service for emergencies, and any that specialize in spot and stain removal. Regardless of what your hotel may claim, experience shows that they frequently can't supply special service in this area.

■ **EMBASSIES**

Embassies are the official representation from a foreign country to the government of the United States. They are all located in Washington, D.C. Many countries also have consulates located in cities around the country. These facilitate business relations with that city and can help your guests with information as well as passport and visa problems.

■ **EMERGENCY TELEPHONE NUMBERS**

This subject heading is for fast reference. Restrict it to the numbers you would need in emergencies. Include in-house numbers such as the hotel doctor and the security department. Remember that your switchboard staff is supposed to have been trained to handle emergency calls and will have telephone contacts that you may not have. Incorporate this list into TELEPHONE NUMBERS so that you have a backup list. Lost pages do happen.

■ **EXERCISE EQUIPMENT (See RENTALS, EXERCISE EQUIPMENT)**

■ **FAX**

The FAX machine has become almost as common as the telephone, and most hotels now provide this service as part of the concierge operation. List the charges for domestic and international FAXes.

■ **FERRYBOATS**

Ferries are a major part of the transportation system in some cities. In addition, they are tourist attractions. In New York, for instance, the Staten Island Ferry is one of the best ways to see the famous skyline. And one of the cheapest ways for a tourist to do so. Your book should include all of the basic data, including hours and schedule.

■ **FILM DEVELOPING**

Tourists will frequently ask where they can have their film developed quickly. All cities now have shops specializing in one-, two-, or three-hour developing services. Be sure to list the ones nearest to the hotel. You may want to list some that are further away if they can offer some special service. Again, hours are the primary consideration.

■ **FLEA MARKETS**

Flea markets have a real attraction for tourists. They will be more difficult for you to list because they frequently have no name, just a location. There may or may not be a telephone number to call for information. You will have to watch the ads in the newspapers, ask your friends if they know of any, and then visit the markets to see what they are like. If they have no names, list them by location. When you visit be sure to find out their hours. If you can't find the organizer of the market, ask several different people in order to confirm that your information is correct.

■ **FLORISTS**

There might be a flowershop within the hotel. If so, get to know them, how they operate their business with regard to your guests, what they can supply, and their level of quality. They will probably have an arrangement with the hotel allowing them to charge deliveries to guest rooms. That is a great convenience but does not guarantee the quality or uniqueness of the floral arrangements. Also record basic information about the very best florist in town. You will need at least one florist who is open when everyone else is closed. Some cities have twenty-four-hour florists.

■ FOREIGN CURRENCY EXCHANGE

Although your hotel may do a limited amount of currency exchange for its guests, it will not do so for the general public. You will therefore be asked for the names of independent companies in this business. Keep only the best-known in your book. If there are any at the airport, be sure to list them because then foreign guests can get rid of their American dollars before leaving the country. Most of the independent money exchangers also offer several methods of transferring money to and from other countries. All of these companies provide brochures that you may use as handouts for your guests. Be sure of their locations because they are frequently in office buildings rather than street-level storefronts.

■ FORMAL WEAR (See RENTALS, FORMAL WEAR—MEN/WOMEN)

■ FOOTBALL

Guests who want to know about a football game need: a schedule of games, including starting times; where the game is to be played; how to get there and back; and tickets (for the latter see TICKETS). Call public relations for the teams and they will be glad to send you schedules. They can also tell you exactly what public transportation serves their stadium.

■ FORTS

If you live in an area that has historic forts, you will be asked for directions to them. You may also list these as SIGHTSEEING if you prefer. List basic information only and get brochures from the agency that maintains the forts, probably one of the parks services.

■ FREE ACTIVITIES

Tourists who are traveling with their families are always looking for ways to keep within their budgets. They will ask your advice about things to do that are free or inexpensive. In these situations it is very handy to have a special subject heading to turn to. Most of the entries on this list will already be under other headings, and it is simply a matter of spending some time reading through your book to duplicate the entries that fulfill your requirements. For example: museums ask for donations but normally do not have a set admission charge. A small donation is acceptable. In addition, they almost invariably have certain hours that are free to the public, frequently at night when other sightseeing is impossible. You will find free events listed in the local newspapers. From your own knowledge of your city you should know where there are street fairs, flea markets, and street performances.

■ **GALLERIES (See ART GALLERIES)**

■ **GAMBLING**

Gambling used to be a dirty word in this country, and only Nevada was available as a gambler's haven. Now, with more and more states revising their laws to accommodate gambling, it is much more widely available. Your list may include the hotels and casinos in your own or nearby towns, riverboats, or such things as the locations of the nearest lottery ticket sales offices and off-track betting parlors. For most of this you will need only basic information. In the case of the casino-hotels, you may want to carry information about their entertainment and special deals designed to attract tourists. In all cases addresses and methods of transportation are vital.

■ **GARDENS**

Gardens, like museums, are a specialized form of sightseeing. They attract both avid gardeners and tourists. They are both centers of learning and oases of peace and beauty to refresh the soul. For all these reasons they are special places and deserve special treatment. They will probably find a place on your FREE ACTIVITIES and SIGHTSEEING lists. You will have to be the judge as to whether gardens deserve their own list. Keep in mind that on your other lists the entries are alphabetized and the gardens will be separated.

■ GAS STATIONS

List only the gas stations closest to the hotel and all of the twenty-four-hour stations you can find. Also list any that may have mechanics on duty at other than normal hours. There won't be many. All you need is accurate basic information.

■ GAY BARS

Experience tells us that guests looking for gay bars normally know where they are. You may, however, have an occasional request for them, particularly from foreign guests. Pick up one of the gay publications at any newsstand and copy the basic data from all of the advertisements and any special listings they may have. We have found that the employees of a good gay bookstore can be a storehouse of information and are willing to share it. If you have no personal knowledge, check your entries with a gay friend or fellow employee.

■ GOLF COURSES

Most private courses will not take your guests. There are some, however, that will. There are two ways to find out about golf courses; read the Yellow Pages looking for advertisements that tell you that their courses are available to nonmembers or go down the list and call them. Private clubs are normally in out-of-the way places, so be sure to get exact directions. They will probably be accessible only by car—be sure to check for public transportation. Call the parks department for information about the public courses. Be sure to find out about reservations policies, the difficulty or challenges of the courses, how many holes, and costs. Also ask the private clubs about dining facilities.

■ GOURMET FOODS

This should be a very short list of the very best retail shops selling real gourmet foods. They will normally have take-out prepared foods as well as packaged items and special ingredients.

■ **GYMS/HEALTH CLUBS**

Most hotels of any size have their own facilities. Should they not, you should treat this subject heading just as you did AEROBICS CLASSES. You will also find that a lot of guests are runners. Be ready to tell them the best nearby place where they can safely run early in the morning. Information about jogging paths in the parks will be available from the city Parks Department. Remember, however, that you and the hotel are liable should the runner be attacked.

■ **HAIRCUTS, MEN**

Your hotel may have a barber shop. If not, find the ones nearest to your hotel and add the best the city has to offer.

■ **HAIRCUTS, WOMEN**

Again, your hotel may boast its own salon. If not, experience tells us that your guests will want only the best. Call and ask the managers for a tour of their facilities so that you know what you are recommending.

■ **HEALTH CLUBS/GYMS (See GYMS/HEALTH CLUBS)**

■ **HELICOPTERS (CHARTERS, TOURS, SIGHTSEEING)**

While helicopter services can be split into three divisions, the same companies generally do all three. It may be easier for you to keep them all under HELICOPTERS and to add notes as to what they provide. Eliminate any that do not have an absolutely reliable safety record. Check with the companies to see whether any of them have arrangements to provide transportation between downtown locations and major airports for the airlines. This service may be available for first- and business-class travelers.

■ **HELIPORTS**

If you are going to recommend helicopters, you must know where they take off and land. Don't forget to find out about public transportation from your hotel to the heliport.

■ HOCKEY

See BASEBALL. (Different sport—same data requirements.)

■ HORSEBACK RIDING

Check the Yellow Pages for a list of all of the nearby stables and riding academies. Call the Parks Department for the locations of any public stables. Add all of the basic data to your list. Be sure you know whether they use western gear or English saddles. Do they have classes? Be sure to have the costs and hours.

■ HORSE RACING (See RACETRACKS)

■ HOSPITALS

As a hotel employee, you will not be called on to determine the hospitals used in emergency cases. This information is for guests who have some reason for visiting a particular hospital. You need only the basic information, but be sure it is accurate.

■ HOTELS

A list of all of the local hotels is invaluable. If your hotel is overbooked, your management may ask you to call other hotels to find space for guests who cannot be accommodated. Your guests, particularly when major conventions are in town, will want to meet or visit their colleagues at other hotels. All that you need to record is the name, address, and telephone number.

■ HOUSES, HISTORIC

Historic houses are not just old houses. They are a physical manifestation of our national heritage. They represent people and lives that are important in the development of our nation. The guests who want to visit these places do so because they have a need to reach out and know more about their past and their roots. If you are lucky enough to work in a city like Boston, you should be prepared with all of the basic information about these houses and have some knowledge about them and their former inhabitants. Being able to intelligently discuss such important attractions is the hallmark of the real professional. It isn't just about names and addresses.

■ ICE CREAM

Although not important in all cities, there are some places (Boston, for example) where ice cream is of overwhelming importance. If only for your own indulgence, you should know all of the best places and the many varieties one can sample. (If you have the normal cravings for sugar and butterfat, researching this will not be a hardship!)

■ ICE SKATING

Nothing is as magical as ice skating in Central Park in New York or on The Mall in Washington, D.C. on a snowy night beneath the stars. It is reason enough to always know the best places to send your guests. Be sure you have all of the costs, including skate rentals. It helps to know at what times adults can skate without children underfoot.

■ JAZZ

Jazz is still a major attraction. List all of the major spots and all of the basic data. Be sure to use your technique for clipping the performance schedules from the newspapers in order to keep abreast of the current offerings.

■ KENNELS (See also VETERINARIANS)

It is not unusual for guests to be accompanied by their pets. Although a number of states prohibit pets in guests' sleeping quarters, others have no restrictions against this as long as guests understand that they are responsible for any damage. Check your Yellow Pages in order to compile a list of full-service kennels. The ones with pickup and delivery service and a full-time, on-premises veterinarian are preferable.

■ **LATIN DANCING (See DANCING)**

■ **LAUNDRY (See DRY CLEANING/LAUNDRY)**

■ **LIBRARIES**

You will be surprised at how seldom you are asked for information about our major repositories of culture. List all of the basic data and be sure to check the hours of operation.

■ **LIMOUSINES**

Limousines are a big moneymaker. In the better hotels, limos fall within the domain of the concierge, and it is understood that you will receive a percentage of the business you send to limo companies. This is one of the sources of income you have to supplement your regular salary. Management favors this arrangement since it costs the hotel nothing and gives the concierge more leverage in terms of getting limos from a variety of sources. Limousine companies will be among your most useful vendors, so be sure to get the best and to develop a strong relationship with them. Even if your hotel has a service it uses, it is important for you to have a backup.

■ **LIQUOR STORES**

Liquor in hotels is quite expensive and, in the less expensive hotels, you will always have requests from guests for the nearest liquor store, where they can buy a bottle for a fraction of the hotel's room-service price. Keep a list of two or three of the nearest with basic information. Try to find one that is open late and on Sunday.

■ **LOST AND FOUND**

Taxi companies, buses, trains, and airports have special telephone numbers for their lost and found departments. When you call, their service people will verify that the objects in question are there and will tell you where they can be claimed. People frequently lose their possessions, especially on the airlines. All you need to record are the names of the companies and the telephone numbers of their lost and found departments.

■ **MALLS (See SHOPPING MALLS)**

■ **MARINAS (See RENTALS, BOATS, or YACHTS)**

■ **MARRIAGE LICENSES**
It may not be needed often, but when it is, it's important to the guest. List the information about how and where one can be married in your area. Include all of the necessary requirements such as proof of age and blood tests.

■ **MASSAGE**
List only the professionals and be sure they are bonded. Include not only their telephone but also their beeper numbers. When guests need a massage, they usually want it as soon as possible. Any reputable practitioner will respond very quickly or will recommend another equally well-qualified person who is available. Massage practitioners will frequently offer you a free massage to acquaint you with their services and abilities. Be aware that there are different types of massage (Swedish, shiatsu, etc.), and your guests will often ask for a specific style. This will help determine whom you call.

■ **MESSENGER SERVICES**
Messenger services are used for local deliveries. Businesspeople frequently need things picked up or delivered, and a personal messenger is the fastest and most secure way to achieve this. Include two or three of the best companies and their fees. One of your considerations is how fast the company responds to your requests. Be sure to use only bonded companies.

■ MONEY MACHINES

Almost all banks will have some type of Automatic Teller Machine (ATM) available to the public. List only the ones closest to your hotel. Be sure you know what systems (NYCE, CIRRUS, etc.) they can access and whether they are open on a twenty-four-hour basis.

■ MOVIE THEATERS

Movie theaters are not frequently asked for ... guests can see movies at home or in their hotel rooms. Keep an alphabetical list by name and add the address and telephone number. Do not attempt to keep track of schedules of movies to be shown since they change every few days. You may want to clip the movie section from the local paper to have available for the occasional guest who asks, "Are there any good movies in town?"

■ MOTELS

List only the best in various price ranges. It is highly unlikely that you will need this information unless you are in a city where the quality of motels rivals that of the hotels. In that case, you might find it of use when your hotel is overbooked and the front desk has to walk people. If you don't use this list over a period of time, eliminate it or give it to the Front Desk Manager.

■ MUSEUMS

Museums and sightseeing attractions have complex basic information. It is important that it be accurate or it will be totally useless and a source of embarrassment. It is not that there are so many new pieces of data to record but the fact that some of the pieces can be complicated. In addition to name, address (include cross streets), and telephone number, be sure you have all of the following:

Hours of operation
You may have to list each day separately. Some museums will close and then reopen at a later hour. Be sure to list the days they are closed.

Admission Fees

These have become very complex. Sometimes there are set admission fees one must pay and sometimes there are "suggested fees" that are supposedly guidelines for voluntary contributions. There is nothing one can do about the former . . . you pay or you don't get in. With the suggested contribution, however, one can give as little as a penny and still be admitted. This can be a boon for a family. In any case, you must know, and record, whether the admission fee is set or suggested. There are also usually "free" times when some corporation has underwritten the costs of keeping the museum open and visitors do not have to pay. These hours are usually in the evening and, since other sightseeing attractions may be closed, it is a good time to visit. Don't forget to duplicate museums with free times under the FREE ACTIVITIES listing. Regardless of whether the fees are set or suggested, they are almost certain to be broken down by adults, children, students, senior citizens, etc. You need all of this information. List the categories and the prices.

Transportation

Many museums are located in areas that are curiously isolated from the best transportation systems. Your guests may have to do some walking. Keeping in mind that a taxi solves this problem easily, you should record the numbers of all of the buses and subways serving each museum. You will also need to know which of these has a station or stop near your hotel. Find the very best method of public transportation to each museum. Your guests will ask you for this information constantly so get it right the first time. Keep in mind that your guests are not always going to specific places directly from the hotel. They may ask you how to go to a museum after they have gone shopping at a major department store. If you have recorded all of the bus and subway stops at the museum, you can refer to the appropriate maps and determine quickly what public transportation will be most efficient from whatever location they may choose to leave.

■ MUSIC

You will need a general category to contain all of those hard-to-classify musical societies, performances, and miscellaneous groups. Even major symphony orchestras may fall into this list. Try to use it as little as possible because it is always easier to find things when they are in a specialized category. You will want to record all of the basic data, including any pertinent performance information you may not have in some other listing.

■ NEWSSTANDS

Tourists will frequently want a newsstand that carries their hometown newspapers or foreign publications. They also often need a twenty-four-hour newsstand. List only basic information, possibly with a note as to what they handle.

■ NIGHTLIFE

Absolutely the worst thing to try to keep track of . . . everything changes all the time. Nightlife falls into many categories such as bars and dancing (of various types), nightclubs, and theaters. You should be able to list them under their most appropriate heading. Try not to use such a nonspecific term as "nightlife."

■ NOTARY PUBLIC

If you are not lucky enough to have a Notary Public on the property, list the nearest one (who might be located in a law office or stationery store) and the hours he or she is available.

■ OTB (OFF-TRACK BETTING)

There are some categories that are applicable only to specific parts of the country or particular situations. They still need to be mentioned. Every concierge will find topics of unique importance to his or her property. Off-track betting, for example, is peculiar to New York and perhaps a few other areas. This is a state-run system of betting parlors or offices where one can place bets on various races. Guests will frequently ask for the address of the nearest location. All you need are the ones closest to the hotel.

■ OBSERVATION DECKS

Tourists flock to all of the high places from which they can view their surroundings. Most major cities have buildings using high floors as either observation decks or as bars and restaurants. You should have all of the usual basic information about these places. You may also want to duplicate some entries under BARS and/or RESTAURANTS.

■ OBSERVATORIES

Observatories should be kept separate from SIGHTSEEING for ease of retrieval. You may want to carry this information in both subject headings if that proves to be useful to you. Keep all of the basic data. Be sure to check to see whether these entries are also eligible for your FREE ACTIVITIES listing.

■ OPERA

Opera is a major attraction. You may want to keep a schedule of performances along with all of your basic reference material. Call the public relations office and they will supply you with schedules plus any advertising material they may have that you can use for handouts.

■ PARKS

You will need to know the areas that comprise the most important or the closest parks to your hotel. Your guests who are joggers will enjoy running in the park, and there are frequently zoos or museums located there. The department of parks can provide you with maps and information about facilities within the parks. Keep in mind that parks are not always safe. You will have to exercise your judgment in terms of warning guests about when and where their safety will be in doubt.

■ PASSPORTS

Depending on its size, your community may have one or more United States Passport Offices. They tend to be extremely busy so anyone needing help is well-advised to be there when the doors open in the morning. The staff can provide all of the forms, answer any questions, and process your application for a passport. It will be sent to you later by mail. In case of emergency, for an additional fee, the process can be greatly speeded up. When needed, this is extremely important information to have, and you must be sure it is accurate. Call the U.S. Passport Office and request that they send you complete data regarding their services. For your book, keep all of the basic information including fees. Don't forget any special telephone numbers. Be sure you know who to call about lost or stolen passports.

■ PETS (See KENNELS or VETERINARIANS)

■ PHARMACIES (See DRUGSTORES)

■ PIANO BARS

While you will want to have this data included under BARS, you must also duplicate it here. Your guests will be specific. When they want a piano bar, they will either say that or they will ask for "somewhere quiet where we can have a drink and listen to some piano music." You don't want to look through your entire list of bars to find something for them. Be sure to include the names of any particularly interesting or talented pianists and times of performances.

■ PIERS

This strange-sounding topic can be very useful. More and more cities are converting disused piers into seaside shopping malls. They usually are of great interest and contain shops, restaurants, and tourist attractions. Include basic information only... don't try to keep all of the shops and restaurants here.

■ PIZZA

One of America's favorite and most asked for foods needs its own listing. Have all of the basic data about the nearest and best places. These will not necessarily be the same. Be sure you have accurate telephone numbers because you will be asked for them often. Don't assume that they will all deliver; some don't.

■ PLANETARIUMS

Planetariums are always popular, particularly with children. Frequently they are a part of a natural history museum, and admission to one may affect admission charges to the other. Keep all of the basic information. Call the public relations office and arrange to receive brochures to use as handouts.

■ POLO

Depending on the clientele of your hotel, you may have requests for basic data concerning polo. It's an elitist sport, and the people who ask for your help will probably be quite knowledgeable about it. What they will need from you is the location of the club where the matches are held, the time of the matches, exact directions for getting there if they are driving, and a limousine if they are not.

■ POSTAGE

Visitors from foreign countries frequently have no idea of the cost of postage. List both domestic and overseas rates for letters and postcards and approximate delivery time. Be sure to keep your information up to date because postal rates change almost every year.

■ POST OFFICES

List the locations of the main post office, the nearest ones, and any that might have extra long or special hours.

■ RACETRACKS

The owners of racehorses have to stay someplace, and it might be at your hotel. If not, you will sometimes have guests who will ask, so be prepared to tell them all of the basic things about the tracks in your area. Racetracks are normally on the outskirts of town because of their space requirements. Call the public relations office and they will send you brochures and material that will answer your every question. Don't be surprised to find that racetracks can be very luxurious operations accommodating thousands of people. Be sure you have accurate starting times for the first race and directions to the track.

■ RADIO CARS

Radio cars are an alternative to limousines. They are smaller, usually Lincoln Town Cars, and much less expensive. They share with limos a high quality of personnel and reliability. In short, the only difference between limousines and radio cars is the size of the car and its amenities. This means that when you have a guest who doesn't want to pay the price for a limo, use a radio car.

■ RADIO STATIONS

Guests will call and ask, "What station carries classical music?" or, "What's the news station?" Your local newspaper lists radio stations by call letters and gives their number on the dial. Clip this information and store it in your Black Book.

■ RAILROADS

Depending on the number of railroad companies and stations serving your city, this could become an involved list. Start your list with the names and basic data of the railroad stations. Then alphabetize your entries by railroad name. Treat each entry in the normal fashion but, if there is more than one station, add to your basic data the name of the railway station used by this railroad. You will need complete information about schedules, directions for getting to the station, phone numbers for reservations and the lost and found departments. Fares change frequently and are best handled by calling the railroad.

■ RECORDS/TAPES

List the stores carrying the largest and best selections as well as the ones nearest your property. In your comments analyze which give the best value for the money.

■ RENTALS

Almost everything can be rented. Listed below are the types of things that are normally requested by guests. You will need to tailor this list to fit your own requirements. Like the rest of the book, it is designed to be used, not to be a test of your ability to accumulate data. If you don't need an entry or certain information, leave it out...if you find subject headings that you do need, add them. Regardless of what you add, you will need to record the same basic information you have already learned to use. You will find that the starting place in your search for information is almost always the Yellow Pages of the telephone book. Some concierges use the Yellow Pages exclusively instead of developing their own book of information. They have a very shallow knowledge of their craft and limited information about the services available for their guests. Don't fall into this trap. It's easy for a concierge to get by; it's very hard work to be really good. Don't forget the importance of your personal notes. Refer to Chapter 5 for complete instructions on how to deal with rental companies.

Audio Visual

Many hotels have their own equipment available for use within the hotel. In case they don't, keep the names of a few companies that give the most reliable service on short notice. Be sure they deliver and pick up equipment. Keep track of prices because they vary considerably.

Automobiles

This list will be used a lot. List the names of the rental companies in alphabetical order. Each of these entries should be followed by as many of that company's local offices as you think you will need. Be sure to include airport locations. Each office should be followed by its address and telephone numbers. Rental fees change constantly so don't make that part of your basic data.

Bicycles

Bicycles are most likely to be requested if your property is near a park where one can ride. There may be rental shops operated by the parks department of the city, or some enterprising person may be renting bicycles from the back of a truck. The latter seems to be a stable type of business and is always to be found at the same location. They will probably want a guarantee while you use their equipment. This may take the form of a cash deposit, a credit card, or they may ask to keep your driver's license until you return. The major problem with collecting data about privately owned shops is that they seem to go out of business with annoying frequency.

Boats

This list is for boats of the size that people, usually one or two, can operate themselves. Canoes, sailboats, and small motor boats may be requested by your guests who are on holiday. Start your investigation by referring to the Yellow Pages. You will also sometimes find this sort of information in local magazines and newspapers. Watch for special articles just before tourist season starts. If your city has a public lake or river frontage, there may be boats rented by the Parks Department. Once you have your list, keep only basic information.

Computers

Be very careful with computer rentals. Try to limit your activity to providing guests with the information about who rents them and let the guest negotiate his or her own rental. They can be extremely expensive, and may require many technical details that you are unlikely to know. It can be very difficult to act as a go-between for this type of transaction. This applies to all types of computer peripherals. Again, the Yellow Pages and local newspapers are a good place to start. It helps to find places with long and weekend hours.

Costumes

Pick the ones with the widest variety and biggest stock. If there are any in your city, they will be listed in the Yellow Pages and almost nowhere else. Keep a few brief notes as to their stock. It can vary quite a bit.

Exercise Equipment

Your hotel may have its own health club that satisfies this need. If not, guests will usually just ask for a stationary bicycle. Again, the Yellow Pages are your best starting place. Be sure you find companies that deliver and pick up.

Formal Wear—Men

In addition to being listed in the Yellow Pages, these companies frequently advertise. It's a lucrative business, and there are a number of large chains specializing in providing tuxedos for men. Try to find out which ones have the best tailors and be sure they deliver and pick up.

Formal Wear—Women

There are more and more shops that will rent cocktail dresses and evening gowns for women. The process may be a little more trouble (sometimes they require several fittings) but this can be a really important service. When you check the Yellow Pages, be sure to look at the entries relating to brides and bridal gowns. These places offer complete services for weddings and often this can include just what you are looking for . . . they don't just deal in wedding gown sales. You won't find many of these places, but you only need one.

■ STROLLERS

Call the places that advertise that they rent everything. A lot of them carry strollers. This is a seldom-asked-for item, but sometimes people don't want to carry a stroller on an airplane. You will have to find one for them to use while they are in your hotel. It happens often enough that hotels have their own. Some also have car seats for small children.

■ REPAIRS

Unfortunately, since we live in a "throw-away" civilization, there are very few people who know how to repair anything. You will find, however, that with a little work you can find them. The Yellow Pages are helpful for basic information. But watch the newspapers and magazines for one of those articles where the writer is terribly pleased with himself for finding the last living person who can reweave the moth hole in your suit so that even your mother wouldn't know. These articles are worth their weight in gold to a concierge because the reporter has done your research for you. They are almost always accurate. Call or visit these people (articles always give addresses and phone numbers) and see for yourself. Over a period of time you will find the best people for all of the following. Use the same techniques for all of them and add subject headings if you need them. Camera and luggage repairs will probably be your most frequently requested. Cross-reference each of these topics alphabetically in your list.

    CAMERAS
    CIGARETTE LIGHTERS
    CLOTHING
    GLASSES
    JEWELRY
    LUGGAGE
    SHOES
    WATCHES

■ RESTAURANTS

As students in a hospitality school you are sure to be involved to some extent with cooking and restaurant management courses. But from a concierge's point of view, restaurants achieve a stature you may never have dreamed of. Restaurant suggestions and reservations comprise a major part of the concierge's job. The importance of this subject heading cannot be overemphasized. You must know not only basic information but the owners, Maitre d's, chefs, and probably some waiters. It is absolutely essential that you know all of the best and most-requested restaurants. If you don't, you'll never make it as a concierge. List them by type of cuisine as well as alphabetically by name. Be sure to eat in each and every one. Many will be delighted to invite you and a friend to dine as their guests (this means free; you should leave a generous tip) so that you can become familiar with their restaurant. Be very clear on one thing: the fact that you have accepted free food does not oblige you to recommend their restaurant. This is not a bribe. The fact that you have accepted their invitation gives them the opportunity to prove to you that they are good enough for your guests. If they don't prove that, don't send them your guests. Always remember that your first obligation is to your guests. If they are happy, so is your hotel management. Concierges account for between 10 and 90 percent of many major restaurants' clientele. It is in the restaurant's best interest to provide top quality cuisine and service. If they don't, they won't last and they know it. When you know the restaurant's management and prove to them that you can provide the quality of clientele they need, you will be able to get the preferential treatment that you need for your guests. Your list should include restaurant hours and dress code. Pay particular attention to the good ones that are open late and on Sundays. Also make note of the ones that serve brunch.

■ ROCK N' ROLL

Guests will often ask you for a specific type of music, and it may be easier, depending on the amount and variety of entertainment your city has, to have separate subject headings for the ones easily identified. Keep the complete list of basic information including cover charges and minimums.

■ SECRETARIAL SERVICES

While your hotel may provide this service, and you may be able to provide some service yourself, it is important to have the names of some good outside companies for the times when your normal facilities are not sufficient. List hours and rates. Remember that costs change after normal working hours and on weekends. Keep notes on which ones will pick up and deliver material and which ones can provide staff to work on-premises with guests.

■ SECURITY GUARDS

Most concierges will never need information about security guards. In cities such as Los Angeles, New York, and Washington, D.C., however, one may be called on to provide personal bodyguards for VIPs. Normally anyone who needs this sort of protection travels with his or her own team of professionals, but even they can get sick or need reinforcement. Convention exhibitors sometimes rent security guards to watch their displays.

■ SHIPS

If you are in an area served by cruise lines, you should know where they dock, how to contact the ship when it is in port, and how to call the Coast Guard or Harbor Master to ascertain arrival and departure times. If you need to contact a ship at sea, call the cruise line's office for the phone number and then dial your long distance operator and ask for the marine operator, who will take it from there.

■ **SHOESHINES**

Any hotel with a barbershop probably also provides shoeshines . . . but not necessarily. Also, all hotels don't have barbershops. Seek out all of the places in the immediate vicinity that might provide this service and get all of the basic information.

■ **SHOPPING MALLS**

List location and directions for getting there. If possible, list the best of the shops in each mall. Don't forget their hours.

■ **SIGHTSEEING**

This category shares with restaurants the honor of being the most sought-after information. Your alphabetical list of entries will include names, addresses, telephone numbers, and hours as well as detailed breakdowns about times of operation, public transportation, and admission charges (remember how you handled MUSEUMS). Anything with free admission times should be duplicated under FREE ACTIVITIES. Your notes should contain a brief explanation of what there is to see. This subject heading is made more complex by the fact that certain groupings of information should be duplicated elsewhere in order to improve your ability to quickly retrieve required data. For people who ask about helicopter tours, historic churches, museums, observation decks, parks, or zoos, for example, it is easier and faster to provide your guests with information if it is all together. You don't have time to sort through every sightseeing attraction in your city in order to tell your guests about the three or four museums they will have time to visit. Experience will tell you which subcategories within SIGHTSEEING actually benefit from having their own subject headings. When you correct or update material always try to think of where else you may have that same entry or data. All subject headings must be kept up to date. Be sure to contact selected public relations offices for material to use as handouts. You must be selective because you will probably not have enough storage space at your desk to accommodate advertising material for all sightseeing attractions.

SELF-EDUCATION/CONTINUING EDUCATION

■ SINGLES' BARS

Basic information plus a few brief notes about the clientele is all you will need for this category. Be sure to duplicate all entries in your master listing called BARS.

■ SKATING (See ICE SKATING)

■ SKYSCRAPERS

While this may be a useful subject heading in Chicago, San Francisco, or New York, it may have limited value in Butte, Montana. Use your own judgment. If you include it you will need only basic information.

■ SOCCER

The guidelines for soccer are the same as for BASEBALL.

■ SPORTING GOODS

List only the best and most complete stores. Add notes so that you know which ones handle a wide variety of equipment and which ones are specialists in a particular sport such as golf or tennis.

■ SPORTS BARS

The same procedure that you have used for other specialized bars . . . basic information plus your notes. Duplicate under BARS.

■ SQUARES

If you work in a city like Boston, where squares are used as addresses, you will need to know where they are. As you compile the material for your Little Black Book, you will find that many entries use the name of a square as their address. If they don't identify its location through the use of cross streets, call them and get exact information about the streets surrounding them. Guests can become hopelessly confused by knowing only the name of a square that is seemingly unrelated to anything.

■ **STADIUMS**

List the names, exact directions for driving and parking, and all of the public transportation available. Include costs for public transportation and the schedules. Be aware that sometimes special trains and buses serve games and events held in stadiums. Call the public relations departments of your transit authority and the teams or groups using the stadium for assistance.

■ **STORES/SHOPPING (See also SHOPPING MALLS)**

The list of stores can be enormous, so concentrate on the best or the ones that provide unique items. Gradually eliminate the ones that are never asked for. Guests who are used to the very best will probably know the names of the most fashionable places and will need only hours or locations. Your notes for each entry should reflect what they sell and the quality level. A separate list by type of store can be useful, unless you know who sells what. This greatly increases your maintenance work, however.

■ **STREET GUIDE**

In New York, Madison and Fifth Avenues run parallel. However, 600 Madison Avenue is at 58th Street, while 600 Fifth is at 49th. It's essential to have an instantly available chart telling you where specific addresses are located. This is a very good reason for always carrying the cross-streets with every entry you make. When you give an address to a guest always add "that is between ___ and __ streets." It greatly simplifies their lives.

■ **STROLLERS (see RENTALS, STROLLERS)**

■ **SUBWAYS**

The concierge should have a stock of maps that are available from the city transportation department. These may come in a variety of languages to accommodate your foreign guests. Subway systems vary considerably depending on the city in question. There are major differences, for instance, between those of New York, Washington, D.C., or Boston. Aside from the questions of cleanliness and efficiency, some have a record of safety while there are others you will want to advise your guests to avoid. The time of day or night and the specific guest destination may determine the safety level. Costs and individual systems for buying tokens or passes are different in each city. Be aware of the costs and the method of payment for subway rides. Also be aware of when it is as cheap to take a taxi (several people times the subway fare may be more expensive than sharing a cab ride). Know the hours of operation for your subway. Not all of them run twenty-four hours a day, seven days a week. If possible, try to keep up with construction work on the system.

■ TAILORS, MEN'S

Have a brief list of the best tailors. Their names are available through the Yellow Pages and the occasional article in magazines or newspapers. You may want to include the names of a few dry cleaning establishments that can oblige with fast service in terms of cuffs on pants or adjusting a waist size. Keep in mind that in a pinch there may be someone on the housekeeping staff who can help.

■ TAPES/RECORDS (See RECORDS/TAPES)

■ TAXI COMPLAINTS

Our experiences show that this is a lost cause. The lost and found telephone number is all you need to start the ball rolling, but the person taking the call is not interested in your complaint. He or she will send you a form to fill out. That is probably the last you will ever hear of it. If the cost of a taxi is comparable to a radio car, and if you have enough advance warning to call one, use the radio car.

■ TAXIS

List a few of the best and most reliable companies who will respond to telephone requests. Again, in many cities there are also radio cars, which are similar to small limousines. These are usually quite reliable and can be used as a delivery service, if necessary. They are always preferable to taxis.

■ **TEA/COFFEE (See COFFEE/TEA)**

■ **TEAROOMS/SERVICE**

Many of the most luxurious hotels now serve high tea in the afternoon. Guests love it, and it is a useful item to include in your book. Don't feel bad about sending guests to other hotels; it won't affect your rooms division business, and it implies a certain confidence in your own establishment to be able to recommend another hotel for a specific service. Always try to suggest a comparable or better hotel than your own because guests then link your hotel image in their minds with the one you recommend.

■ **TELEGRAMS**

Telegrams are almost a thing of the past. Telephones and FAX machines are much more efficient, and telegrams may be mailed instead of hand delivered, causing delays. The Yellow Pages lists them under Western Union. If you don't want to list this, just remember to call information and ask for the central Western Union office.

■ **TELEPHONE NUMBERS**

This is a good place to list all of those numbers you use all of the time or the ones that don't fit anyplace else, like the hotel dentist. You should also duplicate your emergency telephone number list here so that you have a backup. Try to control the length of this list or it will become unwieldy.

■ **TELEVISION STUDIOS/PROGRAMS**

Tours of studios are listed under TOURS, or TOURS, TELEVISION STUDIOS, depending on the number of entries you have. You will find it easier to list PROGRAMS under TICKETS, TELEVISION SHOWS.

■ **TELEX**

Most concierges never have to use a telex machine. When the need arises there is sure to be someone in the reservations department who can help you. You will find the FAX machine a friendly alternative.

■ **TENNIS**

Include all of the best courts, both public and private, that will take your guests on a onetime basis. Remember that reservations are always required.

■ **THEATERS**

All you need is an alphabetical list because guests always ask for them by name. They usually want only the address and directions. You have to find these fast because guests are almost always running late or are nervous about being late. Published phone numbers for reservations frequently reach a central clearing house for tickets, and you will probably have your own source for buying tickets.

■ **TICKETS**

Television Shows

Be sure to get complete information about TV shows from the station in question. In New York the waiting time can be one to one-and-a-half years with tickets available only by mail. When there are tickets available on the day of performance, there are special procedures about how to get them. Call the individual stations for information.

Theaters

Commissions on ticket sales can be a major source of income to a concierge but it is an area that is fraught with danger if sales are not handled correctly. Your hotel may have a special salesperson who handles tickets; in this case your income goes way down. If you handle ticket sales, be sure to work with your supplier at the very beginning to determine exactly how to handle them. Nothing makes a guest madder than having problems with his theater tickets. You should be aware that when there are mistakes you may have to pay for the tickets. One mistake with a pair of tickets could cost you $200 or $300. In your book, you should record the names of your supplying companies, their phone numbers, and the names of your contacts. You will find exact directions for ordering tickets in Chapter 5.

Sporting Events
List the phone numbers for the box offices but also determine whether tickets are available through your normal theater ticket sales source.

■ TIME ZONES
A world map showing time zones is essential; people really will ask, "What time is it in Hawaii right now?"

■ TIPPING
This subject is covered in detail in Chapter 9.

■ TOBACCO
In spite of medical warnings people still smoke. Keep a list of the best and the nearest tobacconists. Basic information is all that is required.

■ TOPS OF BUILDINGS
This list may be redundant since it may duplicate OBSERVATION DECKS. Use your own judgment as to which is more useful to you personally. You may want to eliminate one list or you may choose to keep them both.

■ TOURIST INFORMATION
List Visitors and Convention Bureaus and any information booths that are of use to tourists in your area. Be sure addresses and phone numbers are correct. Meet with representatives from these organizations to determine what they can do for you and your hotel. What brochures and information do they have that you want?

■ **TOURS**

Include a list of all of the different types of tours available. You should also have a collection of descriptive brochures that will be provided by the tour companies. Most of them pay a commission to the concierges for booking tours. The procedure for booking tours is covered in Chapter 5. Cross-reference each of these topics alphabetically in your listing.

> **BOAT**
> **BUS**
> **DAY TRIPS**
> **HELICOPTER**
> **MOTION PICTURE STUDIOS**
> **TELEVISION STATIONS**
> **TROLLEY**
> **WALKING**

■ **TOWED CARS**

List the phone number and the location to which towed cars are taken to be stored. Make note of the approximate amount that it will cost your guests to retrieve their cars. Be sure to know whether payment must be in cash, certified check, or whether they will accept credit cards.

■ **TOYS**

Most of the traveling public is over fifty years of age. When they travel, they frequently buy gifts for their grandchildren. Your TOYS list will be used year-round, not just at Christmas. Be sure to have an extensive list of the best and nearest shops, and any shops featuring antique toys or trains. Electronic toys are also in demand. Remember that department stores have large and comprehensive toy departments.

■ **TRAVEL AGENTS**

It can be very helpful to list a few dependable agents who can arrange tickets and have them delivered to you on behalf of your guests.

■ **TUNNELS**

Tunnels, like bridges, are used by locals as landmarks. Tourists, however, have no idea where they are. You should list these alphabetically by name and add the streets connecting with both ends of the particular tunnel.

■ **TUXEDOS (See RENTALS, FORMAL WEAR—MEN)**

■ **TWENTY-FOUR-HOUR ACTIVITIES**

Like FREE ACTIVITIES, you can gather this information from the entries you collect for other subject headings. Every time you have an entry for something that is open twenty-four hours a day (or close to that if you choose) duplicate the entry here. If someone asks you for a restaurant open at 4:00 A.M., this list should have it.

■ **UNIVERSITIES/COLLEGES (See COLLEGES/UNIVERSITIES)**

■ **USO (UNITED SERVICE ORGANIZATION)**

The USO was established to help members of the armed services who are in strange cities. They provide a multitude of services, many of which are similar to those provided by a concierge. You should know where the local branch is and how to get there. Many of the people who ask for this information will not be guests in your hotel but will walk in off the street for help . . . see that you have it available.

■ **VETERINARIANS (See also KENNELS)**

Guests frequently travel with their pets. You must have available a list of the best vets in the area. Guests may quibble about the price of a hotel room but they don't complain about the cost of a vet when their dog is sick. Find the best, the closest, and the ones who are open twenty-four hours a day. Most major cities have large and efficient animal hospitals that never close; be sure they are on your list. Make notes about what kind of animals a vet will be able to care for. . . some of them specialize in birds or exotic animals.

■ **VISITOR INFORMATION CENTERS (See TOURIST INFORMATION)**

■ **YACHTS**

This is one of those luxury items that you will have little call for, but when you need it you'd better know what you are doing. List only the very best and be sure to go check them out to see what they provide. List approximate costs and call for specific needs.

■ **ZOOS**

Addresses, admission prices, hours of operation, and transportation are the important ingredients in this listing. Refer to the MUSEUMS subject heading because the breakdown of these simple sounding requirements can be complicated.

Some Subject Headings that May Pertain Only to You

Specific Place Names

NEARBY TOWNS

AREAS OR DISTRICTS
Areas of your town that people ask for. For instance, Greenwich Village in New York or the Back Bay in Boston.

SCENIC DRIVES

WHARFS

TOPICS FOR REVIEW AND DISCUSSION

1. Discuss the importance of self-education and continuing education.

2. Discuss various sources you might use to gather material for your Little Black Book.

3. Discuss how a guest calling prior to his or her visit is a good sales opportunity.

QUESTIONS

1. Why is it important for you to have a comprehensive knowledge of your city?

2. What kind of maps do you need to stock for guests and where can you get them?

3. What directions should you always have written out for guests?

4. How do you find out about the attractions in the neighborhood of your hotel?

5. What is the point of having a Little Black Book?

6. Do you have to visit everything listed in your book?

7. How important is the name of a contact?

CHAPTER 8

SERVICES PROVIDED
BY A CONCIERGE
(IN-HOUSE)

General Information and Directions

Within the hotel, the concierge must know the names and locations of all meeting rooms, the hours and dress codes of its restaurants, and the hours of any special vendors (hairdresser, barber, gift shop, jeweler, etc.). It is not necessary to memorize this information, but we strongly suggest having it as the first page of your personal Little Black Book for *instant* access. Ideally, each concierge desk should receive a Daily Event sheet from the banquet department. This lists each function (i.e., AMA Meeting, Chalmers Wedding), its hours, and the room in which it is being held. This is one of your most important pieces of information, and should be treated accordingly. The department we've seen function most effectively keeps the "Daily" on its own clipboard, keeps the clipboard on the wall (or in a specific spot on the desk), and insists that it be returned there after consultation. There is nothing more frustrating than searching for the Daily that one of your colleagues has borrowed "just for a minute" while impatient guests wait to know what room their meeting is in. It gives an extremely poor impression of the hotel whose staff, presumably, knows what is going on.

Mail

The procedures for dealing with mail vary from one hotel to another. Some hotels have a Mail and Package room to sort and deliver it. At others, it falls to one of the clerks at the front desk to sort mail and leave "on arrival" messages. And in some properties, the concierge sorts all the mail. Let's deal with the last scenario, since it affects the concierge.

Mail falls into three general categories: hotel departments, permanent residents, and transient guests. All hotels have rooms where department heads get their mail. While you may leave most departments' mail in their slot, it's always a good idea to deliver the General Manager's mail to his or her office personally.

You will soon become acquainted with any permanent residents at your hotel, and their mail can be slid under the door of their apartment. If they receive a package, leave a note saying that you are holding it for them to pick up.

Mail for transient guests presents a special challenge. Seasoned travelers may advise their correspondents to mark all letters, "Hold For Arrival On (Date)," but we have unfortunately found that this is the exception. Your desk area should have a compartment with pigeon holes for alphabetically sorting and storing mail. Check the computer (or your guest list) to see whether the guest is already in-house or is yet to arrive. If the guest is in-house, write the room number on the envelope and send it to the guest's room. The method of delivery varies from hotel to hotel. For guests yet to arrive, type a note into the computer (or put a note on their folio) that they have "Mail with the Concierge." You will frequently find that "mystery letters" appear—a letter addressed to someone for whom you do not have a reservation. In many cases it's a matter of a reservation being made under the name of a different party from the one on the letter. Having these sorted carefully and accurately, you will be able to happily accommodate those guests who have registered as "Martins" and come to you and ask, "Any mail for "Burghoff?" These letters should be sorted through once a week. After a reasonable amount of time (a month) has elapsed, mark them "Return to Sender" and mail them back.

Packages sent by delivery services are frequently delivered to the receiving room, sales or conference services offices, or to the security guard at the employees' entrance. While they may call you, it is advisable to check with them periodically to see whether there are packages for your guests. Guests at luxury hotels will sometimes have mail collected for them on a yearly basis. Be sure that it is stored in a safe place. Occasionally, guests will leave a forwarding address for mail that may be received after their departure. Note this in your log, and be sure that all members of your staff are aware of it.

Packages

Here, again, procedures vary. Some properties have package rooms or mailrooms where guests' packages are wrapped, weighed, and either mailed or picked up by UPS or an express service. Should that be the case, your responsibility is to give them the item to be sent with specific instructions: Should it be insured? Is it a rush? Is a return receipt required? Guests who may have gotten carried away on a shopping spree and suddenly find they have forty pounds of books or nine more sweaters than can fit in their luggage will turn to you for assistance in getting these items home safely. Package room employees keep careful logs noting when items were sent and the cost.

On the other hand, in some hotels, you may have to find a box, wrap the package, and take it to the post office yourself. Here's where your friends in housekeeping will come in handy—they always seem to have boxes around from unpacking soaps, shampoos, and so forth. The photocopying room is a great source for large boxes. Paper is shipped in ten-ream cartons, and as long as you stack the reams carefully, nobody will object to your appropriating the packing box you need. When you return from the post office, have the cashier post the mailing charge to the guest's account as a paid-out.

Escorting Guests to Hotel Restaurants

The reputations of the best hotels are made by the little things that frequently cost nothing but contribute so much to the guest in terms of special attention and caring. Escorting a guest into your hotel's restaurant is such a gesture. It can also assure the restaurant of a certain amount of business. Call the Maitre d' to tell him you are bringing a party of a certain size. Remember that when you leave your desk, for whatever reason, you should try to ensure that it is covered by someone who is competent. Nothing gives a worse impression of a hotel than to find that management uses the bell staff as substitutes for the concierge. Escorting guests is not mysterious, it simply means you walk with the party to the restaurant. This interval of time is a chance for you to chat with them and find out more about them. It can also be an opportunity to tell them about the restaurant (so be sure you know something about it and the cuisine served there). When you arrive at the restaurant, wait in line but be sure the Maitre d' sees you. He knows that you will not leave your post to escort just anybody to the restaurant and will outdo himself in trying to accommodate them. The waiters will probably notice and will also be more attentive than usual. Be sure to introduce your guests to the Maitre d' by name.

Greeting Guests

As we stated earlier, most concierges do not view their profession as a stepping stone to management, but rather as a lifelong vocation. Therefore, after working a year or two at a property, chances are that you will be more familiar with the guests than anyone at the front desk (which has a much higher turnover rate) or in reservations. Guests who return frequently to a property do so for more than just its location. They want to be recognized. They want to be welcomed. In this computerized age, they want the personal touch, and the concierge is the perfect one to give it to them.

When you recognize one of your regular guests entering the lobby, don't be afraid to get out from behind your desk (if physically possible), shake hands, and extend your special welcome. This need not be anything more elaborate than, "Ms. Worthington, it's so nice to have you back with us." Guests love this sort of personal attention. You can then walk Ms. Worthington over to the front desk and circumvent her possible annoyance at being asked, "May I have your name, please?" by cueing the clerk with a question such as, "Charles, would you take care of *Ms. Worthington*, please?" Just this simple intervention on the part of the concierge has accomplished three important things:

1. *Ms. Worthington is happy that she's "back home"* where people recognize her and will see to her special needs.

2. *Charles looks good* because you have clued him in to both the guest's name and the fact that she should be treated as a VIP. The next time she arrives, Charles will remember her.

3. *The all-important first impression is positive.* Studies have shown that it takes only about four minutes for people to make decisions about such matters as hiring, purchasing, and striking up friendships. Even if the airlines lost Ms. Worthington's luggage, her limo had a flat tire on the way in from the airport, and she missed a crucial meeting with an important business contact, she'll feel, "I'm where people will look after me and take care of my every need." Don't underestimate the importance of creating this feeling.

Escorting Guests to Rooms

In a well-run hotel, VIPs are not just handed their keys and directed toward an elevator; it is customary for a member of the staff to escort them to their room or suite. This is not normally a concierge's job. Usually, one of the front desk management staff gets to have the fun. General Managers usually concern themselves only with higher ranking hotel management or celebrities. However, the occasion might occur when you recognize valued guests or other VIPs and wish to give them a special welcome. Keep up a casual conversation en route to the room—it's the ideal time to find out what special needs your guests will have during their stay.

Building Inspections

The concierge will frequently be called on not only to inspect rooms for VIPs, but to inspect the lobby and public areas of the hotel. The latter may even be part of your normal job. Management should provide you with a checklist for this, including such items as ashtrays clean, sidewalk clear of debris, flowers fresh, and so on. Notify housekeeping immediately of items that require action.

Room Inspections

In luxury hotels, the concierge frequently makes room inspections. Sometimes you will be asked to do so, and sometimes you will want to because the incoming guest is a VIP. You may also make an inspection just because you are on the scene, having just delivered flowers or some other special amenity. Room inspections are not difficult to do but must be done carefully. Ask the Housekeeping Manager to show you what they look for. Aside from the obvious things that you can spot easily like unmade beds, filled ashtrays, or a bug in the middle of the floor, you will find that housekeeping has standards you don't know about. When you have occasion to be in a room, always look for flaws or problems. When you find them, call the housekeeping department and, if appropriate, the front desk in order to have an assigned room changed.

Showing Rooms

Showing rooms can be an interesting break in the daily work. It is usually done by one of the front desk, reservations, or sales department staff. There are times, however, when no one in those departments can be spared, and you will be asked to help out. You will perform this task better if you arrange to have someone from sales or marketing show you their techniques: what features they play up and which ones they do not.

The ordinary traveler or businessperson will almost never look at rooms in advance. When people go to the extra effort of looking at a room, it is normally because they want it for a special occasion (honeymoons, anniversaries, etc.). Pick up room keys from the Front Desk Manager, who will have discussed with the prospective guests the type of rooms they are interested in and will have chosen specific rooms of that type. As you take your guests to the various rooms, you have the opportunity to point out the various features of the hotel as well as to find out more about why they are coming to stay. As you pass public rooms, be sure to let them peek in. They are the hotel's most impressive spaces and deserve to be marketed at every opportunity.

When you arrive at a room, knock on the door and announce yourself by saying "Concierge." Open the door, switch on the lights, and stand back to let the guests enter first. There is one exception to this procedure. There are times when you will be given keys to rooms that the front desk computer shows as clean and ready but that actually have not been made up. All you can do is try to block the guests' view of the room, apologize, and quickly close the door. It is never to the hotel's advantage to show a dirty room. It is even more embarrassing if the room is still occupied. Be sure to report these circumstances to the Front Desk Manager.

Assuming that all is well and you and your guests are now in the room, don't be surprised when they head straight for the windows to see what the view looks like. While they are thinking about the view, you should be thinking about what the view can tell them if they are knowledgeable. If the room is on a low floor and overlooks a busy street, it may be very noisy. Guests who have noisy rooms sometimes want their rooms changed in the middle of the night causing room assignment problems and creating extra work for the housekeeping department. You might want to point out, discreetly, that the view is lovely but that sometimes it can become a little noisy on busy nights.

Guests will want to look around at the furnishings and evaluate the size of the room. If you are in a historic hotel and the furnishings are of interest, point this out. Show your guests the locations of minibars, television sets, and room safes, if available. Also tell them about multiple telephone lines and any special electronic equipment capabilities. Most guests will want to see the bathroom. This is your chance to point out your hotel's selection of amenities, which may include hairdryers, telephones, and minitelevision sets in addition to an extensive collection of toiletries. Suites may have additional rooms with distinctive features you will want to discuss.

After showing all of the chosen rooms, escort your guests back to the front desk (or wherever they should go next; it may be to someone in sales). This is the time to give them your business card and speak to them about the services a concierge can provide.If they are arranging for a special event, you may be very useful to them.

Special Amenities to Stock for Guests

All of the following should be kept on hand for emergencies. When lending out bow ties or cufflinks, we strongly suggest that you inform the guest that unless the item is returned, a charge ($15 for bow ties, $50 for cufflinks) will be added to his bill. Otherwise, these small items tend to walk right out of the hotel.

Bow Ties (black, clip-on)

The single most requested item. Ushers at weddings and men attending formal affairs forget them. We suggest that you learn how to tie a *real* bow tie. (You can pick up a brochure at the tie counter of a department store and master this with an hour's practice.) Nothing endears you more to a guest than this simple service. A man preparing for a formal occasion is in a state of panic unequaled by any other situation. There's always another flight; if you can't get tickets to one Broadway show, you can always see another; but a groom can't get into the limo to the church until the tie is tied. Your hotel's Director of Catering may be able to assist with this in emergencies.

Regular Ties

This is an essential for men who may be refused admission to your hotel dining room without one.

Cufflinks

Have two pairs on hand—gold plate or onyx are safe bets and match everything. In the event that someone who is not a hotel guest but happens to be attending a function there wants to borrow these, don't be shy about asking for some security. We've never had anyone balk when we said, "I'll give back your MasterCard when you return these cufflinks." Of course, you are there to be helpful and friendly, but that does not extend to dispensing cufflinks at random.

Medical Kits

In the case of a *real* emergency you would, of course, notify security. But if someone asks for a bandage you should have some available. However, *never* give out any sort of drug—not even a cough drop or aspirin. We cannot stress this strongly enough. As gently as possible, refer your guests to the gift shop where they may purchase items for their own use. This is a delicate point, and it does seem churlish not to lend a few aspirin to someone who complains of a headache. However, technically you are breaking a law by dispensing medication without a license, and the risk just isn't worth it. Once you explain the legal complications, most people understand. If telling them, "I'd love to help you, but I could lose my job for this," doesn't make the point, call the Manager on Duty.

Safety Pins

These are right up there with bow ties in terms of popularity. Keep several sizes. Things rip.

Scissors

People who have just bought new clothes need them to remove tags. Guests wrap presents. Make it clear to the guest that the scissors are a loan and not a token of appreciation from the hotel.

Wrapping Paper and Ribbon
If you stick to something tasteful but very plain, it can be used for all occasions and reduces the stock you need to have on hand.

Sewing Kits
Get these from housekeeping. Buttons that have been on a tuxedo for years will disengage themselves at the most inopportune moments, and last-minute repairs become necessary. Should you offer to sew something for a guest? If things are quiet and the guest is obviously incapable of using a needle and thread, it can be easy enough to help out. If at all possible, have the guest step around to a more private location so he can be spared the embarrassment of standing in the lobby in his shirtsleeves. It also doesn't look terribly professional to be standing at your desk sewing. Don't forget that your housekeeping department may have a seamstress or a maid who is willing to help you.

Shirt Studs
Rarely used, but when you need them, there's no substitute. Again, stress that these must be returned to you or the cost will be added to the guest's bill. They're expensive.

Stamps
Nothing is more aggravating to a guest than buying postcards to send to friends back home and not being able to get stamps. Depending on the size of the concierge desk, you may have a cash box with stamps, or each concierge may be responsible for his or her own. Know the postage rates and be equipped for letters and postcards, domestic and foreign. If you are not fortunate enough to have a runner who can go to the post office for stamps, order them by mail.

Birthday Candles

Lint Brush

Clear Nail Polish
Every woman knows this stops runs in hosiery.

Umbrellas

Management policies vary from hotel to hotel. Some strictly insist upon their return, others view umbrellas as replaceable amenities.

Men's Black Socks

Voltage Converters

Keep adaptors on hand for foreign electrical appliances.

Stationery

Of course the guest has some in her room, but she isn't in her room, she's in the lobby. People meeting a guest may wish to leave a message.

Travel Kits

Many luxury hotels provide emergency kits for travelers whose luggage has been lost en route. These usually contain a toothbrush and toothpaste, a razor, shaving cream, deodorant, and mouthwash.

Equipment and Tools

Airline Schedules

A well-equipped concierge desk should have a copy of the *Official Airlines Guide*. We have discussed in Chapter 6 how to read this. Frequently, guests will simply ask for your copy and consult it themselves.

Atlas

This need be nothing more elaborate than those large and easy-to-read Rand McNally paperback editions. Guests might be flying to their next destination and then renting a car. They'd like to check the approximate mileage they'll have to drive. Occasionally, guests will ask you to plan an itinerary for a few days' excursion. Consulting the atlas will help you and might even remind you of sightseeing attractions you have forgotten.

Delivery Services

Federal Express, DHL, Express Mail, and UPS Overnight have become indispensable to doing business. Your hotel will probably have an account with one of these carriers. If it doesn't, speak to the Controller about opening one.

Guests who use these services regularly probably will arrive with their own pre-printed airbills, listing their own account number. Guests who do not have their own accounts with these carriers have the option of charging this to a credit card or having the delivery charge put on the hotel account and billed to their room as a miscellaneous charge.

If you can arrange to have a daily pickup, do so. Most carriers are only too happy to comply. It's far better to have a courier stop by even when you have nothing to send out than to risk *not* having a pickup because it was a hectic day and you forgot to call it in.

Sometimes, when a guest trusts you with something to send by Federal Express, he's almost putting his life in your hands. It could be a check to clinch a business deal. It could be orders to sell stock. It could be any number of things, and if, because of your negligence, the parcel is not received on time, his fury will know no bounds. Find out the location of the company's office that is open latest. In an emergency, you may need to rush something over there in a taxi.

Incoming Federal Express or Express Mail packages must also be handled with care. Keep a separate logbook with the following information:

- ❑ Date
- ❑ Airbill number
- ❑ Sender
- ❑ Recipient
  Room number (or on arrival)

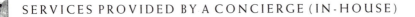

Messengers

For the times when a businessperson has documents or packages to be delivered around town, consult your Little Black Book for bonded messenger services. Be sure to ask the guest by what time something must be delivered. If your hotel does not have an account with a specific company, it will be necessary to call to determine the charge. Process a paid-out in order to get the cash, and pay the messenger when he or she comes by to pick up the item. If your hotel has an account with a messenger service, the charge would be posted as a miscellaneous charge.

Postage Scale

Invaluable for weighing large envelopes or packages to mail for guests.

Maps

Your local tourist bureau or transit authority can supply you with street, subway, and bus maps. Large cities have these available in several languages. Keep an eye on your inventory so that you can reorder before your supply runs out, and have the maps easily accessible at your desk. These are one of the most popular handouts.

Telephone Information

While most hotels have information cards in the rooms explaining the procedure for international direct dialing, most guests never seem to find them. Fortunately, AT&T has printed instructions in several languages and will be happy to provide you with copies. You need only read this information to the guest.

Telex

Although the FAX machine has replaced the telex to a great extent, you may find that there are occasions when you must send a telex. Usually, these machines are located in the reservations department. The variety of these machines is so great, we will not attempt to explain their operation in detail. Ask someone on the staff to give you instruction. Basically, you type a message that is then transmitted to the receiving machine over a telephone line. As the message is transmitted, it prints (original and one copy) on your machine, also indicating length of time the transmission took. Most hotels will bill telexes on the basis of minutes. This is posted as a miscellaneous charge. Send the original to your guest and keep the copy on file.

FAX

Both the savior and the bane of the traveling businessperson, FAX machines make it possible for them to stay in constant written contact with their offices. Should a FAX come in for a guest on arrival, put it in an envelope, place that with the "on arrival" mail, and use the computer to note on the guest's reservation that he or she has a FAX waiting.

Each hotel sets its own rate per page for sending FAXes for guests. Some properties have an elaborate system for logging the day, time, destination, and number of pages of each FAX. Others don't log this information at all. After you have sent a FAX, return the original document and transmittal confirmation to the guest. Post the charges as a miscellaneous charge.

Tour Brochures and Ticket Books

Tour operators (usually boat, bus, or helicopter) will be only too glad to keep you supplied with brochures describing their various services. In some hotels, these tours are handled by a separate concession. Should you be responsible for advising guests and doing the booking, be sure to have the brochures in an immediately accessible location. (Pigeonhole slots along the desk are ideal for this.) Familiarize yourself with the variety of services offered, paying particular attention to the very small print that indicates on what days and at what times the tours run. We have described in Chapter 6 the actual mechanics of taking the deposit and filling out the booking form. Although the commission per tour might be just a few dollars, these can add up very nicely at the end of the month.

Photocopying

In hotels that do not have a business center, the concierge may be called on to make photocopies for guests. It's something all concierges hate. First of all, it takes you away from your desk and prevents you from servicing other guests or answering your

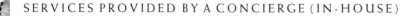

phone. Second, the machines break down, usually on Saturday and Sunday when there is no hope of getting them repaired. However, this is a part of the job that all concierges must deal with.

Each hotel has a set amount that it charges per copy ($.20 is standard). Since photocopying machines differ greatly, we're not going to discuss how to use them. If your hotel's machine is a mystery, *ask* someone to explain its secrets to you. Find out who the hotel's designated "key operators" are. (These are the people who have received the most training on the machine and who can do simple repairs or toner replacements.) Since they are the ones who are called when things go wrong, they'll have a vested interest in instructing you in the finer points of operating the machine.

When the job has been completed, total up the charges, write up a miscellaneous charge, and give it to the cashier for posting.

Zip Code Directory
Travelers love to send postcards. While they might remember Aunt Sally's street address, they frequently forget the Zip Code. You can come to their aid.

Hotel and Travel Index
An invaluable resource for anyone in the hospitality industry, this mammoth book lists hotels worldwide. Whether your guests ask you to book them into "The best hotel in downtown Cincinnati," or to alert the Dorchester in London that they'll be arriving two days earlier than scheduled, you'll find all the information to fulfill these requests at your fingertips: hotel's name, address, phone and FAX numbers, number of rooms, and price range. Frequently there are pictures of the hotel and its facilities. Should your guests need some information on another city (this could range from wanting to know the best restaurant in Dubuque to which Parisian district a certain street is in), you'll be able to consult the HTI, contact a concierge there and get the answer you need.

TOPICS FOR REVIEW AND DISCUSSION

1. Discuss some of the reasons it is important for a concierge to know what is taking place within the hotel and where it is happening.

2. Mail can present many possibilities for errors and problems. Discuss mail systems and try to pinpoint some of the reasons for this.

3. Discuss some of the advantages of escorting guests to rooms.

4. Why should building inspections be an ongoing part of every employee's job?

5. Discuss the reasons for having a photocopier and FAX machine near the concierge desk.

QUESTIONS

1. What is the Daily Event sheet?

2. Name ten amenities to stock for guests and tell why they're important.

3. What is the correct procedure for sending an item by Federal Express?

4. What is the difference between a messenger service and a delivery service?

CHAPTER 9

TIPS AND COMMISSIONS

9

People tip in order to get more and better service. It's a time-honored system that works. People also tip because they are genuinely appreciative of the extra effort you have expended on their behalf. And some people tip as a matter of course. Upon entering the hotel, they introduce themselves to the concierge and tip you lavishly just in case they might need your services at some point during their stay. Hotel management takes tips into consideration in setting wages for all employees who are in a position to receive gratuities.

There is no subject that professional concierges are more reluctant to discuss. Tips and commissions can easily double the income of a good concierge. These extra sources of income vary considerably from hotel to hotel, sometimes because of the clientele and sometimes because of management policy that limits concierges' duties. The best concierges are to be found in the hotels and resorts where the management makes it possible for them to earn as much as they can from their efforts to provide service. These are the establishments boasting a monied clientele who are aware of the value, to them, of appropriate tipping.

What Should Concierges Be Tipped For?

Concierges are normally tipped for handling the following:

- ❑ Restaurant reservations
- ❑ Limousines
- ❑ Ticket sales
- ❑ Airline reservations and tickets
- ❑ Chartering yachts and airplanes
- ❑ Mail or packages
- ❑ Delivering things to rooms

- Sending FAXes
- Making photocopies
- Typing
- Providing special amenities
- Ordering and returning tuxedos
- Renting special equipment

Commissions

Commissions are also a major contributor to the income of a concierge. You will generally receive commissions on the following:

- Limousines

  Limousine companies usually pay a 10 percent commission.

- Radio Cars

- Restaurants

  Restaurants will sometimes pay a commission to the concierge for referring guests to them. Concierges must be sure that they do not let the promise of personal profit affect their judgment of restaurant quality. Your reputation is more valuable to you than the remuneration. Remember that the best restaurants do not need to pay for referrals; their problem is that they have too much business.

- Tickets

  Theater ticket agents will pay a set amount per ticket (usually $2 or $3), and this can add up to a tidy amount since tickets are a very popular commodity. Frequently, it will be necessary for you to utilize your personal contacts in order to acquire tickets to "sold out" shows. These tickets will usually cost several times the face value and are hard to find. In order to compensate for the extra effort required, it is accepted practice for you to add a fee to the price you charge your guest.

❑ **Tours**

The deposit that guests pay when booking a tour with you is your commission. The balance that they pay at the tour office is kept by the company.

In some hotels the management uses outside vendors who rent space in the lobby, usually adjacent to the concierge, for selling tickets, renting cars, providing limousine service, and arranging tours. These vendors not only pay rent to the hotel, they may also pay a commission to the hotel. Since this drastically affects their income, most experienced concierges avoid these hotels.

Tips have no effect on the hotel's income at all, and any commissions that might be received are a tiny part of the total income from the hotel's main profit centers. Therefore, they constitute an inexpensive way for the hotel to provide adequate compensation to a very valuable employee. A concierge will almost never make as much in gratuities as either the bell or door staff, although the concierge's job is much more demanding and complex.

In some hotels, the concierges pool their tips. This is a good idea only if all concierges contribute the same amount of effort to earning them, and if they are all scrupulously honest.

A problem that deserves to be mentioned is that of the Chef Concierge who receives tips from guests who expect that it will be divided among all of the concierges. It frequently is not, and the knowledgeable guest will tip each concierge personally.

Occasionally one will have a guest who brings presents to the concierge instead of tipping. This can be a refreshing and touching experience. The fact that the guest has taken the time and made a special effort to bring a gift can be much more rewarding than money.

The most desirable concierge positions are in luxury hotels where the clientele is likely to tip generously.

TIPS AND COMMISSIONS

TOPICS FOR REVIEW AND DISCUSSION

1. Discuss the concept of tipping.

2. Discuss the role of commissions as they affect a concierge's income.

3. Name the types of things you think will generate the biggest tips.

QUESTIONS

1. Name some possible services that you as a concierge will perform for which you will normally get tipped.

2. Where are the most desirable concierge positions? Why?

3. Why are tips and commissions a way for the hotel to increase the concierge's income without added expense?

4. How do hotels benefit when concierges are able to increase their income via tips and commissions?

CHAPTER 10

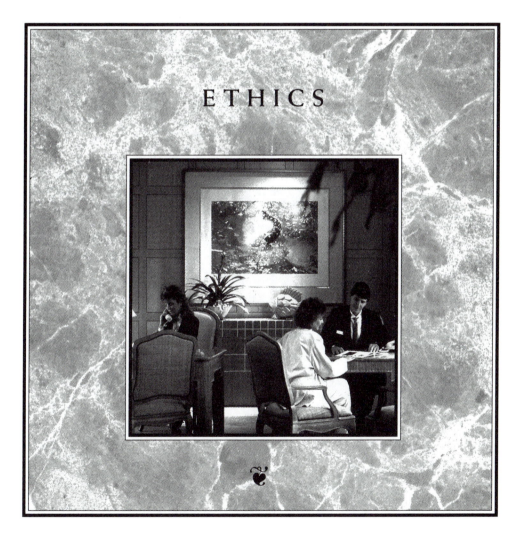

ETHICS

10

Guest/Concierge Relationships

The relationship between concierges and their guests is both a straightforward business relationship and one with complex psychological overtones. This is because the concierge, whom the guest hardly knows, is being entrusted with information and chores the guest considers highly personal. Concierges become the alter ego of their guests and must be able to function on their behalf. In order to do this, concierges become confidants and are privy to information that the guests do not always feel comfortable divulging. Concierges do their best work when they have enough information to know what their guests are really attempting to do. The situation can be delicate, and it is the experience of working together repeatedly and successfully that enables both partners in the relationship to feel comfortable. How you, as a concierge, deal with this problem will make or break your reputation.

Even in the daily requests for relatively ordinary things, you will find it necessary to know something about the guests' financial situation and frequently to have access to their credit card numbers. You will be required to charge things to their account within the hotel (sometimes without their prior authorization) and will know who they are meeting with and why. All of this is very privileged information and must be kept confidential, sometimes even from your fellow workers.

There is always the danger of abusing your position by becoming too friendly or involved with your guests. Remember that while you are their personal representative, you are also an employee of the hotel and in effect, their servant. In short, you must know your place and not overstep the bounds of good taste. You must also be aware that, as an employee, your first obligation is to your hotel. You must never perform a service for a guest that endangers the reputation of your hotel or leaves the hotel libel for a complaint or lawsuit. The classic example of this is when dealing with a guest who asks for information about escort services. There are no services of this sort that can be recommended safely, and the repercussions can be disastrous. Concierges are also frequently asked to join a guest for dinner or drinks after hours. Never do this. Not only does it change your relationship with the guest, it is also against all hotel rules and can lead to instant dismissal.

When you begin working with guests, you may find them shy and reticent about asking for your help. Aside from the reasons we have already touched on, keep in mind that they might not be accustomed to using concierge services and might not know what you can do for them. One of the duties of the concierge is the education of guests in the use of hotel services. Don't be shy about making suggestions as to things you can do for them or that other departments in the hotel can provide. Also be sure they realize that you can handle most of the details of their entire trip, including networking with other hotels on their itineraries and liaisoning with their offices. The more they know about what you can do for them, the more they will ask of you.

A good concierge is one of the reasons guests choose to return time after time to a hotel. The job is not an easy one, and if you have the necessary skills to perform the duties required and the social skills to deal with the guests satisfactorily, you will be qualified for much higher positions within the hospitality industry. Those who choose to remain concierges do so because there is a satisfaction in dealing directly with guests that is lost as one moves into management.

What Are the Hotel Rules?

At the orientation session, you will be given a list of your property's rules and regulations. Depending on what part of the country you're in, the size and nature of your property (resort, convention hotel, airport, or other), and its labor relations climate, this list can range from one page to a dozen. You will be responsible for abiding by these rules— any infringement can lead to disciplinary action. While the exact rules are property specific, they generally fall into these major categories:

1. Hygiene (including, among other things, hair length, appropriate makeup, general cleanliness, amount of jewelry, elements of grooming, importance of wearing a clean uniform)
2. Pilfering
3. Drug abuse and drinking
4. Discretion

Common Sense and the Golden Rule

The longer you work as a concierge, the more involved you may become in your guests' private lives. It takes a while for trust to be established. It must never be violated. In an age when housemaids, chauffeurs, and secretaries are writing memoirs about the indiscretions of the rich and famous, the concierge remains true to professional standards. In addition, a good concierge generally has genuine affection for the guests. Betraying their confidences would be unthinkable.

In terms of dealing with your colleagues, keep in mind the Golden Rule: "Do unto others as you would have them do unto you."

This covers a wide range of behaviors:

- ❑ Arrive on time if you want to be relieved on time.
- ❑ Keep accurate records.
- ❑ Be helpful—share your information.
- ❑ Be flexible.
- ❑ Don't gossip.
- ❑ Above all, be scrupulously honest in your financial dealings with your colleagues.

ETHICS

TOPICS FOR REVIEW AND DISCUSSION

1. Discuss how ethics affect the guest/concierge relationship.

2. Discuss how the need for complete information from the guest and the need for discretion on the part of the concierge interact.

3. What ethical issues are involved in trying to overcome a guest's reticence?

4. Discuss the ethical issues involved in having access to a guest's credit card information. How do you keep this information secure yet available for your use?

QUESTIONS

1. As a concierge, where is your first obligation?

2. Why is it bad policy to accept invitations from guests?

3. Under what conditions would you recommend an escort service?

4. Why are hotel rules important?

5. What are the most important things to keep in mind when dealing with your colleagues?

CHAPTER 11

HOW DO YOU BUILD YOUR REPUTATION?

The main ingredient of any concierge's reputation is hard work. You must constantly expand your store of information, provide an excellent level of service to guests, and always strive to have the right answers and solutions to problems.

But, by itself, hard work will provide only a limited reputation, and you owe it to yourself and your property to expand on that.

Having reached the level where your guests, hotel management, and your fellow employees think you are wonderful, it is time to think about the outside world.

Remember all of those vendors of services discussed in Chapter 6? They should also be singing your praises by now. You will have sent them a lot of business and will have done so in a competent and professional manner. You will have made a point of visiting the restaurants and stores to which you direct many of your guests, meeting the owner and manager. Your guests receive even better attention now since those in charge know you personally.

With this record of success behind you, it is time to broaden your horizons. This is an opportune time to become active in concierge organizations.

Local Concierge Associations

If your city has a local concierge organization, you should join it as soon as you start your job. It will provide you with the opportunity to meet the other concierges in your city and to attend special "concierge parties" at local restaurants. Even at this early stage in your career you will find it useful to start networking with your colleagues. Now that you have some experience behind you and are ready for new challenges, you might want to campaign for one of the elected offices or to work on one of the committees that take on special projects. These activities will not only give you high visibility within the organization but will be really enjoyable.

Clefs d'Or

In 1929, Ferdinand Gillet and ten other head concierges founded the U.P.P.G.H. (Union Professionelle des Portiers des Grand Hotels), more commonly called the "Clefs d'Or" because of the crossed gold keys insignia concierges have usually worn on the lapels of their uniforms. The members of this organization pledged to help one another and were so successful that in 1952 Mr. Gillet organized the U.I.P.G.H. (Union Internationale des Portiers des Grands Hotels), an international Clefs d'Or. Headquartered in Paris, it contains over 4,000 members in twenty-four countries. Approximately 150 members are from the United States.

Les Clefs d'Or USA, Ltd. functions as an association of professional concierges in the United States and acts as an affiliate of the U.I.P.G.H. Its purpose is to establish and promote high professional and ethical standards, and generally to coordinate, promote, and assist the activities of concierges; to foster friendship and communication among concierges of hotels in the United States and throughout the world; to expand the training of those entering the profession and, in general, to promote, foster, enhance, and improve the technical skills and professionalism of concierges. It fosters the development of both the hotel industry and tourism in general and strives to maintain the highest possible standards of service for hotel guests (see Figure 11.1).

Membership is limited to concierges who are employed by hotels and resort hotels having a transient clientele and who work full-time at a desk located in the main lobby of these hotels, from which they provide services to all the guests of the hotel. Concierges who work exclusively on VIP floors or those employed in office buildings, apartment complexes, or private clubs do not quality for membership in the Clefs d'Or.

The Fact Sheet that Les Clefs D'Or USA sends to prospective applicants further states that they must be at least twenty-one years of age, of good moral character, and employed in the hotel industry for at least five years, three in the position of concierge.

When he or she has met these qualifications, a prospective member submits a two-page application form (see Figure 11.2), a 1" x 1" portrait photograph, a photograph of the work area showing his or her desk, and at least two letters of recommendation from members of Les Clefs d'Or who are not on the membership committee.

Les Clefs d'Or USA, Ltd.

(Member U.I.P.G.H.-Paris)

<u>PRINCIPLES OF PROFESSIONAL PRACTICE</u>

PREAMBLE

Our profession is a calling which requires application of specialized knowledge and courtesies for the benefit of others. The profession of the concierge endeavors to promote the highest standards of conduct and integrity in professional service and in our activities as an organization. The Les Clefs d'Or U.S.A. (herein, Les Clefs d'Or) has identified several professional principles for emphasis.

In considering these principles, it should be remembered that these or any other statements about the profession of the concierge are not all-inclusive, are subject to interpretation, and are subject to change.

In approving the Ethical Principles, Les Clefs d'Or believes that maintaining the standards and principles set forth in this document can make a substantial contribution to the service of the profession and its members to hoteliers and guests.

ETHICAL PRINCIPLES

By setting out several basic ethical principles for the concierge, Les Clefs d'Or seeks to encourage courteous, honest, reputable and reliable professional practice. Our profession depends on these attributes. Concierges should strive to reflect these characteristics as an expression of dedicated concierge service.

The concierge should have pride in his or her professional endeavors. The obligation to act professionally calls for higher motivation than that arising from concerns of civil liability or other penalty. Being a concierge carries a significant responsibility to others and all concierge services should reflect this recognition. Each concierge should make every effort to ensure that his or her services are used properly.

* A concierge should neither practice nor permit discrimination on the basis of race, color, sex, age or national origin.

* A concierge should not condone, engage in or defend illegal conduct or practices.

* Les Clefs d'Or members and non-members should be treated on a reasonable, non-discriminatory basis. Les Clefs d'Or members should not disparage non-members or others. New members should be encouraged.

Figure 11.1 Clefs D'Or – Principles of Professional Practice (photo of Clefs D'Or document)

* A concierge should conduct all matters in a professional,
polite, courteous and helpful manner to guests, fellow workers
and colleagues; a concierge should not be defiant, rude or
discourteous to others.

* Professional conduct demands timely and courteous response to
all correspondence, inquiries, and phone calls, as well as
prompt payment in full of all transactions handled by the concierge.
Commitments to colleagues and others should be honored; if
circumstances prevent honoring previous commitments, it is courteous
to notify the other person immediately.

* Personal problems should not interfere with the professional performance
of a concierge. Accordingly, the concierge should refrain from
undertaking any activity in which a conflict is likely to lead to
inadequate performance or harm to an hotelier, guest or colleague.

* A concierge should not misuse his or her position or authority.
A concierge should not demand goods, services or money as compensation
for his or her own personal gain. A concierge should exercise objective,
independent judgment in the evaluation and recommendation of goods
and services.

We should always keep in mind the purpose of our positions is to serve
our guests and the purpose of our membership in Les Clefs d'Or U.S.A. is to
serve each other through friendship.

Vive Les Clefs d'Or!

Figure 11.1 (cont'd) Clefs D'Or – Principles of Professional Practice (photo of Clefs D'Or document)

Membership in the Clefs d'Or can be the key to one of the world's speediest networks. International conventions are held yearly. In addition, they have local meetings at which members constantly share information—and contacts.

Les Clefs d'Or USA, Ltd.

(Member U.I.P.G.H.-Paris)

APPLICATION FOR MEMBERSHIP

(Please Type or Print)

LAST NAME:_____ FIRST NAME:_____ INITIAL:_____

TITLE:_____ HOME ADDRESS:_____

_____ HOME TELEPHONE NO._____
                                                    (Include Area Code)

HOTEL NAME:_____ HOTEL ADDRESS:_____

_____ HOTEL TELEPHONE NO._____
                                                    (Include Area Code)

HOTEL TELEX NO._____ NAME OF SUPERVISOR:_____

_____ TITLE OF SUPERVISOR:_____

NUMBER OF ROOMS IN HOTEL:_____ NUMBER OF OUTLETS (RESTAURANTS):_____

_____

WHY DO YOU WISH TO BECOME A MEMBER OF LES CLEFS D'OR, USA?_____

_____

_____

_____

_____

_____

ARE YOU A MEMBER OF ANOTHER CONCIERGE ASSOCIATION? YES ( )   NO ( )

IF YES, STATE WHICH ONE:_____

ARE YOU A MEMBER OF A HOTEL UNION? YES ( )   NO ( )

IF YES, STATE WHICH ONE:_____

DO YOU SUPERVISE BELL STAFF: YES ( ) NO ( ) DO YOU SUPERVISE OTHER PERSONNEL? IF

SO, PLEASE LIST: _____

TOTAL AMOUNT OF PERSONNEL YOU SUPERVISE, IF APPLICABLE:_____

DO YOU WEAR A UNIFORM? YES ( ) NO ( ) THE CONCIERGE ARE MEMBERS OF WHAT

DEPARTMENT?_____ HOURS OF OPERATION:_____

_____

Figure 11.2 Clefs d'Or – Application for Membership (photo of Clefs D'Or document)

BRIEF DESCRIPTION OF DUTIES: _____

_____

_____

_____

WHO HANDLES YOUR DUTIES WHEN YOU ARE ABSENT? _____

_____

BACKGROUND:

YEARS IN PRESENT CONCIERGE POSITION: ____ YEARS IN PRESENT HOTEL: _____

LIST PREVIOUS EMPLOYERS AND POSITIONS (For the Past Five Years):

EMPLOYER:_____ POSITION:_____ ADDRESS:_____
_____ DATES:_____ _____
                                MO/YR   SUPERVISOR
_____
    PERSONNEL DIRECTOR

EMPLOYER:_____ POSITION:_____ ADDRESS:_____
_____ DATES:_____ _____
                                MO/YR   SUPERVISOR
_____
    PERSONNEL DIRECTOR

EMPLOYER:_____ POSITION:_____ ADDRESS:_____
_____ DATES:_____ _____
                                MO/YR   SUPERVISOR
_____
    PERSONNEL DIRECTOR

EMPLOYER:_____ POSITION:_____ ADDRESS:_____
_____ DATES:_____ _____
                                MO/YR   SUPERVISOR
_____
    PERSONNEL DIRECTOR

EMPLOYER:_____ POSITION:_____ ADDRESS:_____
_____ DATES:_____ _____
                                MO/YR   SUPERVISOR
_____
    PERSONNEL DIRECTOR

DO YOU SPEAK/WRITE/READ ANY FOREIGN LANGUAGE? YES ( ) NO ( ) IF YES, STATE

WHICH ONES:_____

_____

_____

Figure 11.2 (cont'd) Clefs d'Or – Application for Membership (photo of Clefs D'Or document)

PLEASE ATTACH TO THIS APPLICATION FORM: One 1" x 1" portrait photograph, one photograph of your work area showing your desk, and at least <u>two</u> letters of recommendation from members of Les Clefs d'Or, USA who are <u>not</u> on the membership committee.

I hereby authorize Les Clefs d'Or, USA or any of its representatives to verify any of my employment references. I also understand that misrepresentation or ommission of facts called for is cause for cancellation of membership.

I also hereby acknowledge that if admitted to the Association, I will abide by the Certificate of Incorporation, the By-Laws and the rules and regulations of the Corporation.

DATE: _____   SIGNATURE: _____

Figure 11.2 (cont'd) Clefs d'Or – Application for Membership (photo of Clefs D'Or document)

PAGE 4

<u>APPLICANT IS NOT TO WRITE ON THIS PAGE</u>

MEMBERSHIP COMMITTEE MEMBER MUST COMPLETE FOLLOWING:

NAME OF APPLICANT: _____

CITY/STATE: _____

APPROVED ( ) REJECTED ( )

SIGNATURE OF COMMITTEE MEMBER: _____

DATE: _____ MEMBERSHIP COMMITTEE CHAIRMAN MUST INITIAL: _____

BOARD OF DIRECTORS: APPROVED ( ) REJECTED ( )

SIGNATURE AND DATES:

_____   _____

_____   _____

_____   _____

_____   _____

_____   _____

COMMENTS:

Figure 11.2 (cont'd) Clefs d'Or – Application for Membership (photo of Clefs D'Or document)

Public Relations

All hotel employees, from the door staff to the General Manager, are constantly performing public relations efforts on behalf of the hotel. Few employees, however, share the concierge's opportunities for continual promotional activities . . . and they cost nothing. The concierge has constant contact with a wide range of individuals and will be perceived by them as the hotel's representative. The pride you take in your property, your demeanor, and your professionalism can enhance your hotel's reputation, as well as your own, among all those you meet.

One of your most concrete opportunities to promote your hotel chain will occur when guests ask you to make reservations on their behalf at another hotel. A Four Seasons concierge in Philadelphia wouldn't dream of sending a guest to a Marriott property in Chicago; he'll keep the guest within the Four Seasons network. A Marriott concierge would follow the same pattern and send the guest to another Marriott hotel. This helps not only the hotel chains but also the concierges involved. Once they have established a personal contact they will tend to maintain it. This leads to additional business for the hotels and adds to concierges' personal reputations.

Recently, travel magazines have discovered that concierges make very good copy, and the number of articles featuring interviews with concierges has soared in the last few years. This type of exposure can be wonderful publicity for both you and your hotel, but, if you are chosen as an interviewee, exercise caution. Never mention names of guests. Refer to people for whom you have performed the impossible as "a well-known Hollywood star" or "an international businessperson." And remember that discretion is vital to the reputation of a concierge . . . don't gossip.

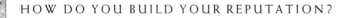

TOPICS FOR REVIEW AND DISCUSSION

1. Discuss the importance of a solid base of achievement and knowledge before a concierge tries to deliberately build an image.

2. Discuss local concierge organizations and how a concierge can benefit from membership.

3. The Clefs d'Or is the major professional organization for concierges. Discuss its purposes and the benefits of membership.

4. Discuss the ways in which hotel employees create good or bad public relations for their property and for themselves.

QUESTIONS

1. How will your guests benefit from your ever-improving reputation with outside vendors of services?

2. When should you join your local concierge organization?

3. What is an easy way to visit some of the local restaurants?

4. Who is eligible for membership in the Clefs d'Or?

5. If a guest asks you for a hotel reservation in another city, what do you do?

CHAPTER 12

CONCIERGE LEVELS

Now that the giant hotel has proved to be such a success, hoteliers are facing a new problem: how to provide service for 1,500 to 2,000 room establishments that would like to cater to both first-class and luxury category guests. The most obvious and successful solution has been the development of the hotel within the hotel—the Concierge Level—a small luxury hotel within a much larger first-class hotel. It sounds simple enough, but there are many problems inherent in this type of marriage. The question of "luxury," for instance, means something different when applied to a first-class hotel from what it does to a small strictly luxury-class establishment. Everything is affected by the size of the property, the management orientation, the quality of personnel, and the quality of teamwork that can be maintained when the team is so large and varied. What is considered luxury by a Hyatt or Sheraton is not necessarily considered to be luxury by the Carlyle or the Plaza Athenee.

Concierge floors have evolved fairly rapidly. In the beginning, they were an attempt by first-class hotels to provide a little better service and accommodations for favored guests and upper-echelon business travelers. Now, however, there is serious consideration being given by some of these companies to upgrading their concierge floors to the traditional concept of luxury. Hotels currently under construction are planning this level of service and designing their physical plants to provide the required facilities.

Everyone knows that the key to luxury is service, and that means a high ratio of staff to guests. In the United States, staff is a difficult and expensive commodity. Some hotels that have tried to add personnel in the form of extra concierges on each floor have subsequently eliminated them. The latest trend, which is beginning to peak, is the addition of amenities to try to compensate for the real service that is too expensive for most hotels to afford. Luxury service also requires a clientele with the style and savvy to demand it. Anybody can spend money for objects. Spending for service is something else.

Regardless of the problems, the trend toward including concierge floors is catching on fast. Marriott, long the favorite of businesspeople because of its many first-class establishments, has been a forerunner with its Concierge Lounges. Other chains such as Hyatt, Westin, Holiday Inn, and Hilton also provide similar services.

Hotels containing both first-class and luxury levels face many challenges in providing for two similar but very different worlds. Upper-level managers must constantly be aware of which level of service they are dealing with and must be able to confront the varying situations appropriately. The major problems are not only in management per se, but in the design of the physical plant and the amount of teamwork that must be generated by management—plus, and this is a big plus, the right staff. Just as there are distinct differences in the clientele for the two areas, so must there be two different types of staffs to support them.

The Physical Plant

All hotels with special concierge floors need a security system to control access to these floors. In some properties, the elevator to the concierge floor will only respond to a guest's concierge floor room key. In others, guests must show the concierge on duty their room keys to be allowed admittance to the lounge.

Once the guest has been whisked to the concierge level, there must be a registration desk and a bellstand with luggage storage facilities. The luggage and package storage areas must be large enough to always function properly. Luggage standing about on the first-class lobby floor is one thing—on the concierge level it is unforgivable. Remember that you are not only providing all of the standard features of a first-class hotel, you are offering something superior for the concierge levels. There must be more grace, charm, efficiency, and personal attention in everything—that's what luxury is all about.

All ho... ...cts and designers are increasingly aware of the many amenities ...he rooms. Jacuzzis, hot tubs, and towel warmers are commonplace. ...e not as aware of the requirements of designing an attractive and ...sk and work area. Although the concierge is the best source of ...sign of this area, he or she is almost never consulted. Thus, for ...m any storage space adjacent to the concierge desk, even though ...ther things for guests is an essential service in a luxury area.

What are the many things that a concierge should be doing in order to satisfy not only the guests but also the management? What tools do you need in order to do these things? What information must you have available and how do you procure and store it? How many concierges work on the same shift and require duplicate facilities? What access do they need to hotel computer systems and guest history? How much shelf space is required for reference material and for the many handouts about the hotel and sightseeing locations? Maps alone require a great deal of space. Secure space is needed for bow ties, cufflinks, bandages, all of the various sizes of stationery, envelopes, Federal Express and other overnight mail envelopes and boxes. There are rotary card files and logbooks. Where should the telephones be placed?

Planners must also remember to provide space for a typewriter, copier machine, FAX and telex equipment. The amount of time saved by your not having to go to another part of the hotel to use these facilities will more than pay for the installation within your own space. If you are alone, it may not be possible for you to leave your desk unattended while you go to make photocopies or send a FAX. In addition, equipment shared by many departments has frequent downtime. Guests are often annoyed by the problems inherent in the lack of such facilities and are livid when told the copier is out-of-order.

Many of the new amenities, such as VCRs, will require storage space if kept in the concierge areas.

And, of course, the question of a sit-down desk for the concierge (which is prettier) versus the standup counter (which is much more efficient) will plague both the architect and the General Manager. There are arguments for both, and, in our experience, appearance usually wins out over efficiency. We also find that guests prefer counters. They didn't stop by for a visit. They want to tell you what they want and be on their way. The concierge should never be fenced in behind his or her work area. You need to be able to instantly walk around the counter or desk in order to greet a guest or to move quickly about the lobby. Location of the concierge is also of paramount importance. Your desk should be located in a prominent position where you can see and be seen by all of the guests as they come and go. There must be enough space for a group of guests to await your services without blocking traffic. If there are frequently guests waiting for service on the concierge floors, more staff is needed.

Staff

The staffing of a concierge department in a large property with a concierge floor will be very different from that of a small hotel where, for example, four concierges might rotate shifts. There are four distinct levels.

Manager

This is the head of the department, responsible for hiring and firing, scheduling, payroll, ordering food and beverages for the lounge, and resolving guests' problems. He or she usually has the least guest contact.

Supervisor

The supervisor performs the manager's duties in the manager's absence, relieves concierges for their breaks, banks concierges working at the registration desk in and out, blocks rooms, runs arrival reports, performs the full range of concierge functions, and trains new employees.

Concierge

In addition to performing all the functions we have described in Chapters 6 and 8, the concierge must be able to check guests in and out, post charges to accounts, and run a cashier's report.

Concierges working on a concierge level tend to see the same guests over and over again. They can spend more time talking to them and have a greater opportunity to develop a working relationship with guests than do their colleagues in the lobby who might deal not only with hotel guests but thousands of people who may be attending a function in one of the meeting rooms.

Attendants

The attendants set up and clear away the breakfast, hors d'oeuvres, and cordials services although, in some hotels, either the concierges themselves or room service perform this function. Hard-working and underappreciated, these employees contribute enormously to guest satisfaction. Concierge levels have come to be equated with "free food" to many guests. People who will wait patiently for a room to be cleaned will turn really nasty if the orange juice is late.

Training

Some hotel chains train their entry-level concierges on the concierge floors. This has several advantages. To start with, the pace on these floors is usually slow, so the new employee will not be deluged by guests demanding instant service. Also, concierges become thoroughly conversant with the full range of duties involved and are well-positioned for advancement to supervisor and, eventually, manager.

Let's briefly review the basics of checking guests in, blocking rooms, and checking guests out.

Checking Guests In

The importance of making a good impression at check-in time cannot be over-emphasized. You are the first or second hotel employee with whom the guests come into contact, and your behavior can color their entire stay.

The actual check-in process can be broken down to the following steps:

1. Verifying the reservation (frequently made under a different name)
2. Confirming room rate and length of stay
3. Having guests sign in
4. Establishing credit
5. Determining room preference (close to elevators, queen- or king-sized beds, etc.)
6. Assigning room (changing status to "Occupied")
7. Making keys
8. Calling the bell staff to have the luggage brought up

It is your job to perform all these tasks accurately and smoothly while keeping up a pleasant conversation with the guest. Initially, you may find it difficult to go through the steps while chatting. Relax. Repetition makes it easier. Remember the first time you tried to drive a car with standard transmission? It seems like there's so much to do at once: ease up on the clutch, let go of the brake, and step on the accelerator. How can you do this with only two feet? You learned that by doing, and you will learn this as well.

A typical guest-concierge exchange might go as follows:

CONCIERGE: Good afternoon, sir. May I help you?

GUEST: Name's Wilson. Checking in.

C: Welcome, Mr. Wilson. We've been expecting you. Is that Mr. George Wilson from Rapid City, South Dakota?

G: Right.

C: Mr. Wilson, you'll be staying with us for three nights, is that correct?

G: Yes.

C: And you were quoted a rate of $225 per night. Is that correct?

G: Yes.

C: Mr. Wilson, would you please verify that this is your correct home address and sign this registration card?

G: Certainly. (Guest signs registration card.)

C: And how will you be settling your account, Mr. Wilson?

G: American Express. Here's my card.

C: Mr. Wilson, we are required by law to let you know how much credit we will be getting on your card. The total will be _____, which represents three nights, plus tax. (At this point you verify credit for that amount.) Do you have any room preferences?

G: Last time I was here, I stayed just around the corner. It was real convenient coming over for breakfast. Do you have anything close to the lounge?

C: Let me check for you, Mr. Wilson. Yes, I do have a lovely king-bedded room very close to the lounge. It will just take a minute to make the keys. Did they give you claim checks for your luggage? Thank you. I'll have your luggage sent up immediately. I know that you've been our guest before, but I'd like to remind you that we serve a complimentary continental breakfast daily from 7 to 9 A.M. The honor bar is set up at noon. You pour your own drinks and fill out one of the forms on the table. The drinks are then charged to your room. In addition, we have complimentary hors d'oeuvres from 5 to 7 P.M. Cordials and cookies are put out at 9 P.M. My name is Helena. If there's anything I can do to make your stay with us more pleasant, please don't hesitate to call me. Enjoy your stay, Mr. Wilson.

While we're not advocating that you memorize a script, knowing in advance exactly what to say will make you less nervous and less apt to forget a step. Note the following from the above suggestions:

1. Greet the guests before asking, "How may I help you?"

2. Phrase your first several questions so that the guests answer, "Yes." This puts them in a positive frame of mind.

3. Use your guests' names.

4. Explain the full range of services offered. (Make Mr. Wilson happy to be paying the extra amount for luxury accommodations.)

It is extremely important to smile at your guests, use their names, and maintain eye contact during this conversation. This may seem like a minor detail, but it is not. The guests want to feel *welcome*. They are disoriented by being away from home and want to be in a friendly atmosphere. Naturally, there will be pauses in this conversation as you get approval on the credit card, search for the reservation, and make the keys. That's the time to inject a remark about the weather, ball teams, or to find out what you, as a concierge, can do for them during their stay. If you are a regular reader of the *Wall Street Journal* and can comment intelligently on the guests' business, do so, but avoid questions like, "How does it feel to be the victim of a hostile takeover?"

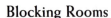

Blocking Rooms

Another function that concierges working on the concierge levels perform is blocking rooms. All guests who are paying the full concierge-level rate should be preblocked. In order to block a room, you bring up the guest's reservation and assign an appropriate room number. The system should provide a space for indicating whether or not the guest has already checked in. This is especially crucial in a sold-out situation, when people may be upgraded to any available space.

Checking Guests Out

This is a delicate time. You must know how to print a copy of the folio, explain any charges the guests don't understand, arrange for credits if necessary, and finally have the guests sign their charge vouchers. Tact and patience are very important. You want the guests' final memory of the hotel to be as pleasant as their first impressions.

A typical guest-concierge exchange might be:

CONCIERGE: Good morning. May I help you?

GUEST: Room 3020, checking out.

C: Certainly, ma'am. Let me run a copy of your bill so that you can check that everything's in order. (This takes a few minutes. Meanwhile, you have learned the guest's name from looking at the computer.) Will you need a bellman to assist you with your luggage, Mrs. Hendricks?

G: Yes.

C: (Calls bellstand.) Please send a bellman to room 3020. Mrs. Hendricks is checking out. (Hands folio to guest.) There you are, Mrs. Hendricks.

G: That looks fine.

C: May I please have your signature on this charge voucher?

G: Sure.

C: Mrs. Hendricks, I'll just staple your copy of the voucher directly to the bill. There you are. I hope you enjoyed your stay with us and that we'll see you again very soon.

Disadvantages of Working on the Concierge Level

Having stated that the concierge level is a fine place for training, we must also point out that a great deal of this training has nothing to do with being a concierge—it is training to be a front desk agent.

The admission requirements for membership in the Clefs d'Or recognize this problem and state specifically that concierges who work on VIP floors are not eligible. There is a reason for this. The most obvious is that you will spend a great deal of time doing clerical work rather than servicing guests. As nice as the lounge might be, it is still completely removed from the daily activities of the rest of the hotel. You are limited to servicing only a small percentage of the hotel's guests. This is, obviously, not the role that professional concierges see for themselves.

When the image of the concierge becomes confused, the guests are uncertain about how to deal with you. They are expecting the concierge to be a professional to whom they can confide their problems and needs. When they find you in the role of a waiter, bartender, or front desk clerk, their confidence is affected. If the last task you saw a person perform was pouring coffee or stacking dishes, would you ask him to plan a special night out on the town for you and your colleagues? Is this the person you would choose to handle your business arrangements? Would it occur to you that he could do all the things discussed in this book?

Special Work Involving Other Departments

Concierges working on concierge levels will interface with other departments more intensively than their colleagues working in the main lobby.

Housekeeping

In the concierge lounge, you will deal with housekeeping differently because you are basically a Front Desk Manager and are responsible for the rooms on your floors. Housekeeping must let you know when rooms are ready, and you must let housekeeping know when someone checks out. Because the concierge lounge is adjacent to the rooms,

the housekeeping supervisor frequently comes into the lounge to provide you with information, rather than calling on the phone. This makes for a more personal relationship. Housekeeping is also responsible for maintaining the lounge area. This becomes a formidable task because you are usually serving food on numerous small tables. This means that there are a number of tables and chairs to keep clean. Because people spill food, the carpets need extra maintenance. You might also have your own bathrooms that require constant cleaning.

Security

Because the concierge floor is deliberately isolated from the rest of the hotel, it must have its own surveillance system and be visited by members of the security department on a frequent basis. Since the concierges have cash boxes, they must be escorted to the front desk by a member of the security department. Unfortunately, since liquor is served in the lounge, guests can become unruly. A quiet word from a large, imposing security man will be much more effective than polite entreaties from the concierge.

Room Service

Room service generally provides all the food that is served at breakfast and cocktail buffets. On the occasions when an attendant is late or a no-show, it may be necessary to prevail upon room service to send someone to assist with the setup.

TOPICS FOR REVIEW AND DISCUSSION

1. Discuss the evolution of concierge levels.

2. Discuss the special ways in which concierges on the concierge level network with other departments.

3. Discuss the chain of command within the concierge level.

QUESTIONS

1. Why do some hotel chains train their entry-level concierges on the concierge level?

2. Why is it important to make a good impression on the guests when they check in?

3. What are the disadvantages of working on the concierge level?

4. Describe the process of checking in a guest.

5. Why is security so important to the concierge level?

GETTING YOUR FIRST JOB

E ventually one's school years come to an end, and one is faced with the prospect of finding a job. Now is the time to evaluate the years just past. What have you learned in school? Have you added any practical experience by working during summer vacations? What are your strong points? In what classes did you excel and what sorts of things did you find most interesting? This information is not just of academic interest, it is vital to the process of eliminating the things you don't like, making it possible for you to focus on those things with which you prefer to be involved. Examining your background, both strengths and weaknesses, helps in the process of constructing a picture of who you are and the type of work you would like to do. This is not difficult and can be of great help to you.

Our experience has been that in contemporary society people no longer feel that they have to settle for only one career during their lifetime. As you work in the hospitality industry and gain experience, you may find that other areas interest you more than remaining a concierge. There is, however, very little evidence that people drawn to concierge work ever leave it for other jobs within the hospitality industry.

There have been many books written about occupations and how to find the proper one. Read these books carefully for the details of how to prepare for interviews and any information they may contain about resumé writing. As a new graduate, you are fresh out of school and have little, if any, actual experience.

Resumé Writing

The purpose of writing a resumé is not to get a job. It is to get an interview. The interview is your chance to prove just what a good employee you could be and to make the interviewer want to hire you. Don't confuse these two steps in the overall process. There are various ways to design and present the information you consider important, but there are some general rules to follow:

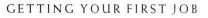

❑ **Keep your resume short—one page if possible.**
Yours is only one of a great many your reviewers must read and they are more likely to read resumés that are concise. Don't overwhelm them with too much information. Save some of your comments for the interview.

❑ **Do not use sentence structure.**
Start phrases with action verbs. Present your material clearly, briefly, and with words that lead the eye from fact to fact.

❑ **Omit personal data, such as age, weight, etc.**
These are facts that can sway judgment against you and distract from the strong selling points you are trying to convey. Information of this type won't help you and could hurt. Leave it out unless it has a strong bearing on the job.

❑ **Start with your most recent job and work back.**

❑ **Mention any honors you have achieved.**

❑ **Mention any office skills you have, especially typing.**

❑ **Mention any computer systems with which you are familiar.**

❑ **Mention any languages you speak, write, or read.**

❑ **Mention certifications such as CPR, first-aid, etc.**

❑ **Mention any sports or hobbies you enjoy that show you are a good team player.**

Letters from Recruiters

Who knows the requirements for jobs better than the people who recruit and hire? In the letters in Figures 13.1 and 13.2, Human Resources Directors tell you, in their own words, what they look for when they interview candidates.

EXECUTIVE OFFICES

Boca Raton
Resort and Club sm

501 EAST CAMINO REAL
BOCA RATON, FLORIDA 33432·6127
AREA CODE 407 · 395·3000
FAX 407 · 391·3183 / TELEX 803·936

February 24, 1992

Mr. McDowell Bryson
223 West 10th Street
Suite 3B
New York, NY 10014

Dear Mr. Bryson:

In our search for the perfect concierge, we have compiled the following list of attributes. One is not necessarily more desirable than the other; rather they all work together to describe what we feel would constitute the ideal.

The ideal concierge would speak at least two languages. In a situation where English is the primary language spoken by the guest, a firm command of the English language would be required, along with outstanding conversational skills. A concierge must possess an innate desire to help other people, as well as be very resourceful. A concierge is expected to be a worldly person, well-informed and well-traveled. An immaculate appearance and a welcoming smile are necessary. The ideal concierge must be tenacious and must handle pressure well. The ability to work well with others is required. A concierge must have a thorough knowledge of the surrounding community as well as a general understanding of hotel operations. The ideal concierge should be familiar with all types of cuisine and should have a broad understanding of what constitutes fine cuisine and a fine dining experience. A concierge should be an extrovert and should take great pride in his or her chosen profession. A good network of relationships with other concierges and community sources is helpful in facilitating guest service. Not least in importance, the concierge must understand and value the concept of service above and beyond expectation.

Keeping in mind our constant goal of the ultimate in guest service, we feel that a concierge who possesses these qualities would best serve our organization in the pursuit and maintenance of our standards.

Sincerely,

Herbert M. Pianin
Director, Quality Control

HMP/mjv

Figure 13.1 Letter from Boca Raton Resort and Club

Dear Prospective Hospitality Professional:

Dedication, commitment, professionalism and service; four words each with individual definitions and meanings, however, when used collectively, begin to describe the attributes that we seek in identifying our guest services representatives.

In order to maintain the meritorious level of service that has become the trademark of the Ramada International Hotels & Resorts Corporation, we seek individuals in our Concierge Department who are 'ambassadors of good will', who have demonstrated an extraordinary commitment to the highest levels of guest service and customer satisfaction and who take personal pride in catering to the business and personal needs of our guest population.

We desire resourceful, knowledgeable and creative team players who are the epitome of professionalism; attentive to detail, responsible, enthusiastic, and who possess the skills necessary to accommodate not only the needs of the seasoned business professional, but those of the neophyte traveller as well. Patience, empathy and understanding are also virtues that combined with a solid background in a customer service related profession, provide the framework necessary to establish the relationships with our guests which are essential in ensuring the satisfied customer.

It continues to be our goal and mission in the hospitality industry to consistently provide an unparalleled level of service. We consider our Concierge Department to be the front runners in providing that service and in assisting the hotel in attaining our goal to remain at the forefront in the travel and tourism industry.

Hospitably yours,

Elin Salinger
Director, Human Resources

RAMADA
RENAISSANCE.
TECHWORLD
WASHINGTON D.C.

999 9th Street, N.W., Washington, D.C. 20001-9000 Tel (202) 898-9000 Fax: (202) 789-4213   ♻ Printed on recycled paper

Figure 13.2 Letter from Ramada Renaissance Techworld

Grooming for the Interview and the Job

You are applying for a job as a professional, and your clothing should reflect this. Men, of course, will wear suits, preferably in a dark color, with subdued ties. Women should also wear suits, sheer stockings, and heels. In the corporate world, business dresses are acceptable for interviews, but the hotel world is more conservative. If you don't own a suit, wear a dress with a matching jacket. If you wear sneakers en route to the interview, stop in at the hotel's ladies' room before going to the human resources department and change your shoes. Have your ensemble in order before you enter the office. Wear little or no jewelry—clanging bracelets and dangling earrings do not make a good impression.

Arrive at the property early enough to look around. How's the noise level? Is there a waterfall or something that you just *know* would drive you crazy? What are the guests like? Do the employees seem happy? Remember that an interview is a two-way street—the property is evaluating you, and you're evaluating the property. Get a feeling for the atmosphere. Don't try to analyze your reaction but listen to your senses. Is this the place for you?

While you're waiting to be interviewed, study the furnishings of the human resources area. Are they promoting a new property? Are they signing up a softball team? Is there a copy of the Annual Report that you can peruse? This will not only calm your nerves, it will give you an opening conversational sentence.

As you progress closer to getting hired, the General Manager will probably interview you personally. Chances are that you will be kept waiting at least a little while in the reception area outside the office. Don't sink into a soft sofa— it's impossible to stand gracefully when your name is called. Choose a straight-backed chair and keep your feet underneath it so that you are ready to move immediately.

Never underestimate the importance of the first few seconds. While waiting, keep your belongings (these may include a purse, briefcase, coat, and umbrella depending on the season and the weather) close at hand so that you can gather them up quickly. Even though you're in a strange environment, you want to show that you're in control.

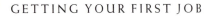

Interviews: How to Enjoy Them and Shine

Everyone is nervous at job interviews. The interviewers expect it. However, by practicing answers to possible questions and role-playing with a friend you can conquer your nerves. Don't think of the interview as an interrogation; look at it as an opportunity to show the prospective employer just how wonderful you are.

When you are introduced to the person who will interview you, whether it be the Director of Human Resources, an assistant, or the General Manager, that person will probably state his or her name and extend a hand. Give a firm handshake, look the person right in the eye, state your name, and say "Delighted to meet you." You will be offered a chair. Sit up straight, looking both relaxed and alert. Keep breathing.

Following are some of the questions that are asked most frequently in job interviews. We've suggested what the interviewer might be looking for and a strategy for answering. Remember to maintain eye contact during the interview and to keep smiling.

"Tell me about yourself . . ."

This is a typical ice-breaker. Interviewers like it because it gives them a good initial "feeling" about you. They figure that if you can't be articulate about yourself, you can't be articulate about anything.

Generally, it isn't so much what you say when you answer this question that's important, it's how you say it. Don't get tongue-tied.

A good way to start your answer might be to come right out and stress a strong point in your personality, showing your natural gregariousness and love of people.

"I love travel and have always been fascinated by other cultures. That's why I speak three languages. And I really like people—I enjoy making them feel as excited at being in this city as I always am and helping them out when they're in a bind. Invariably, when I'm out walking, people will stop me to ask for directions. I guess I give the impression of being well-informed."

The main things to bear in mind are:

❑ Stress only positive features.

❑ Back up general statements with proof. Stress your accomplishments.

❑ Try to key what you've said to the qualifications needed for the job.

❑ Keep it brief.

"There's a lot of pressure in this job. Do you think you can handle it?"

Don't be in too much of a hurry to answer, "Yes." Ask the interviewer to describe the kind of pressure he or she means. Is it long hours? Understaffing? Complaining guests? Instead of bragging about how well you perform under pressure, indicate that pressure has never been a problem for you.

"Where do you see yourself five years from now?"

The interviewer is trying to determine whether you have company loyalty or whether you're going to use his property for basic training and then go someplace else. He is also trying to determine your level of ambition. Are you looking for promotions and advancement or do you want a secure job with limited opportunities?

In answering, stress that you are looking for a property where you can work happily for a long time. "I'm interested in stability, and I've read that this company has a record of treating its employees well. I'd like to be the Head Concierge right here," is an answer no one will argue with.

"What do you consider your major strengths?"

You should never have any trouble with this question. If you know what you're looking for in a job, you know exactly what qualifications you bring to it: good memory, attention to detail, organization, language ability, enthusiasm, and so forth.

"What do you consider your major weaknesses?"

Turn this question around. Transform your "weakness" into a desirable characteristic:

"People tell me that I'm too hard on myself. I guess that's because I'm a perfectionist." "I'm a workaholic." "I'm stubborn. When I set out to do something, I never give up." "I get impatient with people who are lazy."

The interviewer will probably end with: "Are there any questions that you'd like to ask me?"

It doesn't make a particularly good impression to immediately ask about vacations or holidays, but a question about the benefits package (Are both medical and dental

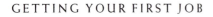

benefits included? How long is the waiting period?) is certainly in order. "What are the possibilities for advancement?" will also cue the interviewer that you are interested in long-term growth within the company.

While you can't come right out and ask for the job, you can convey your interest, eagerness, and enthusiasm. "It's always been a dream of mine to work in a luxury property like the St. Francis. . . . I feel that I have a great deal to contribute and would make a good addition to your staff."

Most likely, the interviewer will thank you for coming by, tell you that they are still interviewing other candidates, and promise to call you in a few days. Exit on a strong note. Shake the interviewer's hand, look him or her in the eye, and say, "Thank you. It's been a pleasure talking to you. I'll be looking forward to hearing from you."

Gather your things and leave. Don't waste the interviewer's time by putting on your coat in the office. Go home secure in the knowledge that you have done your best. And when you get home be sure to write a "thank you" note to the interviewer.

TOPICS FOR REVIEW AND DISCUSSION

1. Discuss why visual presentation can be as important as actual content in a resumé.

2. Discuss the purpose of a resumé and how it accomplishes this.

3. Discuss the types of questions you would like to ask the interviewer.

QUESTIONS

1. In which sequence should your previous experience be presented?

2. What information should you not include in your resumé?

3. How should you dress for an interview?

4. How can you prepare for your interview?

5. What are some of the questions you can expect to be asked?

STORIES FROM
THE CONCIERGES

14

The previous chapters were designed to teach you how to be a concierge: how to function within your hotel environment, how to research and keep your information up-to-date, and how to provide the quality of service for which concierges have achieved a reputation worldwide. This chapter brings you a few of the stories from professional concierges that illustrate the wide range of requests guests will expect you to be able to handle. This is the colorful part of the job, the really challenging things that make all of the daily routine worthwhile. You will soon start your own collection of stories about "impossible" requests and will find that you never forget the guests who bring them to you.

Adele Ziminski, Writer/Former Concierge

On Adele's first day of work at the Barclay Chicago Hotel, the general manager called and asked her to find out Mickey Rooney's favorite brand of pipe tobacco, go to the store, and buy him a pound as a welcome gift. "Sugar Babies" was coming to Chicago, and Mr. Rooney was due to arrive that afternoon. She called the theatrical producers in charge of the touring company, found out the name of the Stage Manager and the phone number of the theater where they were playing, and was able to comply with the GM's request by presenting Mr. Rooney with a pound of Captain Jack Gold within minutes of his arrival.

While working at the Pierre, Adele had a favored guest who was an extremely soft-spoken, low-key businessman from Saudi Arabia. He chose not to give his name when calling, but since the connection was always very staticy and Mr. X had a very distinctive voice, she was always able to address him by name. His requests varied considerably. One time, he asked Adele to purchase two magnifying mirrors similar to the ones in the hotel bathrooms. Since the mirrors cost over $400.00 each, it was handy to be on good terms with the cashiers to get a pre-arrival paid-out. Another morning, he asked for six five-pound bags of Pillsbury XXX self-rising flour to be purchased and boxed so that he could take them on a plane. He was leaving in half an hour. After calling a few local groceries to check their stock, Adele left the Assistant Manager in temporary charge of her desk and taxied to the market and back. By the time Mr. X checked out, she had the flour securely packed and ready.

Not all stories end in triumph. Asked by some dignitaries to determine the time and place of polo matches "somewhere on Long Island," Adele called the sports desks of local newspapers, riding academies, and private clubs (thinking that their members must play polo). No one knew. Months later, it occurred to her to ask one of her cousins, a horse-woman. "Bethpage State Park, Sundays at 3," was the reply.

When we recommend that you think about all your friends and relatives, their occupations and hobbies when dealing with a tough request, we're speaking from experience.

Dilys Lentz, Chef Concierge
The Lancaster, Houston, TX

Dilys's own words say it best:

"One of the many interesting and challenging incidents recently was an attorney who had come in from out of town for an important meeting and traveled light. She forgot to pack her shoes, and arrived in slacks and sneakers. By the time she realized her mistake the stores were closed, and court was in session at 8:00 A.M. That morning I gave her my shoes (it was the first time I had worn them) and I wore her sneakers all day with my uniform. I was a funny sight dashing about the lobby in black dress suit, white dress shirt and tie and sneakers. Then it started to rain. Our guest was out there wearing *my* new shoes. I had her use our limo and driver all day until my shoes were returned. This guest was one happy camper."

Ada Baione, Chef Concierge
Loews New York

At 9:00 P.M. one New Year's Eve, a guest frantically called and confessed that he had neglected to pack dress shoes for the night's formal festivities. Loews Regional Vice President lived on the property, so Ada called and asked him his shoe size. Fortunately it matched the guest's, and he was prevailed upon to lend his shoes for the evening. Ada adds, "I'm married now, and my husband wears a size 9, so I know I can always get a pair of those for a guest."

James Gibbs, Chef Concierge
The Ritz-Carlton, Naples, FL

Guests at the Ritz-Carlton seem to take a particular delight in playing "let's stump James." They always lose. One guest wanted an unusual way to propose to his chosen bride. Never at a loss, James rented a helicopter and the question was popped several thousand feet above the Ritz-Carlton. She said "yes" of course.

On another occasion, an English visitor wanted assistance in finding a set of Mako shark's teeth. James phoned Peru and had an entire shark flown to Naples. Engaging the services of the kitchen staff, he had the head boiled down and retrieved a complete set of choppers.

Jim Gimarelli, Chef Concierge
The Benson On Broadway, Portland, OR

Jim had a guest who had lost a favorite necklace and asked his help in finding it. He called the tour bus company. No luck. He had her room searched. No luck. He called the airport. Again, no luck. As a last resort he called the airline on which she had traveled. They found the necklace under the airplane seat. Another success story for Jim.

Marcelle Cattan, Head Concierge
The Beverly Hotel, NY

During Marcelle's first week on the job she was able to utilize some of her real-life experience. One of her guests from Brazil needed to know where to find a leg bandage for a racehorse. Marcelle, without hesitation, gave him the name and address of an establishment that provided medical supplies for horses, thus beginning her reputation as a wizard. What she didn't tell the guest was that she had dated a man who had an interest in horses and they used to meet in front of the shop.

Good concierges don't just wait to be asked for advice. When they see something wrong they step in to help. One winter's day, Marcelle stopped an Asian woman who was leaving the hotel and explained to her that it was much too cold to go out wearing a cotton shirt and sandals. From then on the woman stopped by the concierge desk each day to be sure she was dressed appropriately before leaving the hotel. On the last day of her visit, the guest gave Marcelle a coin engraved with her own image. She was Queen of a small country near Tibet.

Barbara van der Vloed, Chef Concierge
The Drake Swisshotel, NY

One of Barbara's favorite stories is about a couple from Scandinavia who involved her in their wedding plans. She was originally asked about requirements for wedding licenses and how to find a photographer. Next they asked her to help them with the wedding—to be held that day. She found a hairdresser for the bride, a tuxedo for the groom, and arranged for both the limousine and photographer. She also served as a witness to the ceremony, and threw the traditional rice.

Maria Benvenuti, Concierge
The Grand Hyatt, NY

On a day like any other, Maria was approached by a frequent guest. While visiting in New York he had found a new BMW that he couldn't resist. So he didn't. Now he needed to arrange for it to be shipped to his home in Saudia Arabia. Maria took care of all of the paperwork and had the car picked up at the BMW dealership, then taken to JFK Airport where it was shipped by UPS. It was shipped from New York to Brussels, Brussels to Kuwait and then on to Saudia Arabia. The cost? Only $15,000.

McDowell Bryson, Writer/Former Concierge

While working in the concierge lounge, McDowell was approached by a gentleman who had been attending a convention at New York's Marriott Marquis Hotel. The convention was ending, and he and his family wanted one last super experience in the Big Apple before going home. After running through the list of wonderful things that New York can offer, none of which seemed to appeal, McDowell suggested that the guest charter a yacht for the evening and experience the city from a different viewpoint. The guest loved the idea and handed over his American Express Platinum card. Spur-of-the-moment yacht charters are not as easy as they sound. McDowell found a company that had a suitable boat, and they managed to round up the captain, chef, and crew of sixteen, all of whom had thought they had the weekend off. Arranging for a limo to take the guests to the pier and pick them up on their return was the easy part. The next day McDowell received a call from the yacht brokers saying that the guests had enjoyed themselves so much that they extended their cruise for an extra four hours. With four crew members per guest, they had probably never been so pampered in their lives.

Ben Steyger, Concierge
The Wyndham Hotel, NY

Ben has stories about all kinds of wonderful requests including finding a baby elephant for a family reunion. One of the most challenging was from a guest who accidentally mailed his passport in an Express Mail letter. Ben called branches of the New York Post Office until he found the one responsible for sorting the mail leaving the hotel. It took all of his powers of persuasion to convince a postal worker to call him when the envelope surfaced for processing, but Ben got the passport.

Index

A

Advancement opportunities, 8–10
Aerobics classes, list of, 108–109, 131
Airline personnel, assisting, 45
Airline reservation services, 77–79
Airlines information
    charter service, 110–111
    list of, 109
    schedule information, 172
    shuttle service, 110
Airports, information regarding, 111–112
Amenities
    guest provisions, 35
    special items to stock, 169–172
American concierge, role of, 5
Amusement parks, information regarding, 112
Annual events, assistance with, 112–113
Antiques, information regarding, 113
Apprenticeship training system, 5
Aquariums, reference information regarding, 113
Arrival checking, significance of, 64
Arrivals Report, information provided, 47
Art galleries, current information regarding, 113–114
Attendants, role of, 208
Auctions, list of, 114
Audio visual rentals, current information, 143
Automobile rentals
    arranging for, 84–85
    information regarding, 143

B

Babysitting service, providing, 79-80, 104, 114–115
Baione, Ada, 233
Balloon rides, information regarding, 115
Balloon service, providing, 115

Banquet and catering department, working
    with, 24–25
Bars, information regarding, 115
Baseball/Basketball/Hockey/Soccer, information
    regarding, 116
Beaches, information regarding, 116
Beauty salons, basic information, 116
Bellstand/Doorman, supervision of, 25
Benvenuti, Maria, 235
Bicycles
    rentals information, 144
    trails availability, 117
"Black Book"
    creation of, 106–108
    information contained, 107–108
Blocking rooms procedure, 212
Boat rental information, 144
Bookstores, information regarding, 117
Bow ties, tying instructions, 117
Breweries, information listing, 118
Bridges, location of, 118
Brochures/handouts, necessary supply of, 34,
    112, 141, 155, 175
Bryson, McDowell, 235
Building inspection process, 167
Bus lines information, 118
Business forms, supply of, 34

C

Car service, *see* Radio car service, providing
Cashiers, working with, 19
Cattan, Marcelle, 234
Caviar, providing of, 118
Cemeteries, information regarding, 118
Checking out process, assistance with, 212
Check-in process, assistance with, 18, 209–211
Children's activities, information listing, 119

Chinatown, information regarding, 119
Chocolate, shopping information, 119
Churches, information regarding, 119–120
Clefs d'Or, membership procedure, 194–200
Clothing, shopping information, 120
Clubs, private, information regarding, 121, 130
Coffee houses, information regarding, 121
Coffee/tea purchases, shopping information, 121
Colleges/universities, information regarding, 122
Comedy clubs, current information, 122
Commissions, receipt of, 182
Company Annual Report, information provided, 15
Complaints, handling of, 53–54
Computer rentals, information regarding, 144
Computer system, use of, 63–67
Concert halls, current information, 122
Concierge desk
    design of, 31, 33, 36, 206–207
    location of, significance of, 31–33, 36, 206–207
    See also Concierge floors
Concierge floors:
    design/layout of, 206–207
    disadvantages of, 213
    housekeeping issues, 213–214
    room service, 214
    security required, 214
    staffing, *see* Staff, duties of
    training on, 209
    trend of, 205–206
Concierge organizations, benefits of, 48, 193
Confirmation cards, use of, 67, 87, 93
Consulates, information regarding, 122
Convention centers, current information, 122–123
Convention Sales Department, working with, 43
Costume rental information, 145
Cruise lines, arrangement process, 123
Customs, U.S., basic information, 123

D
Daily Event Sheet
    information provided in, 163
    oversights, 24
Dancing, location recommendations, 123–124
Delis, recommendations of, 124
Delivery services
    information regarding, 124
    providing of, 173
Department stores, basic information, 125
Directions, assisting with, 49–50, 104, 137
Director of Operations, duties of, 17
Discount shopping, basic information, 125
Dolls, information regarding, 125
Downtown, knowledge of, 125
Drugstores/pharmacies, information regarding, 126
Dry cleaning/laundry, basic information, 126

E
Education convention groups, assisting, 44–45
Embassies, information regarding, 126
Emergencies, handling of, 44
Emergency telephone numbers, availability of, 126
Employment search
    interview preparation tips, *see* Interviews,
        preparation tips
    resumé writing, 219–220
    sample letters, 220–222
Engineering department, relationship with, 21
Equipment requirements, 33–34, 36, 207
Escorting guests, 165, 167
Ethical issues, 90, 182. *See also* Guest/concierge
    relationship
European concierge, duties of, 4–5
Exercise equipment, basic information, 145

F

FAX machines, availability of service, 126, 153, 174–175
Ferryboats, basic information, 127
Film developing, information regarding, 127
Flea markets, location information, 127
Florist, basic information, 127
Flowers
    ordering process, 95–97
    storage provisions for, 35
Food and Beverage department, duties of, 15, 17, 22, 24
Football, basic information, 128
Foreign currency exchange, information regarding, 128
Foreign language, command of, 8, 23–24, 46
Formal wear rental, basic information, 145
Forms, computerized, 64–67
Forts, basic information, 128
Fraternal organization conventions, assisting, 45
Free activities, knowledge of, 128–129
Front Desk Manager, duties of, 17
Front office, working with, 18–19

G

"Gallery guides," as information source, 114
Gambling, information regarding, 129
Gardens, basic information, 129
Gas stations, basic information, 130
Gay bars, information regarding, 130
General Manager
    duties of, 15, 18, 167
    working with, 109
Gibbs, James, 233
Gimarelli, Jim, 233
Golf courses, information regarding, 130
Gourmet foods, shopping information, 130

Greeting guests, 166, 211
Ground floor services, 32–33
Guest/concierge relationship
    abuse of, 187
    formation of, 46–47
    hotel rules and, 187–189
    trust development, 189
Guest education, 51–52
Guest history records, information contained in, 41–43, 47, 54
Guest relations, four basics of, 46
Gyms/Health clubs, information providing, 131

H

Haircuts, basic information regarding, 131
Helicopter services, availability of, 131
Heliports, knowledge of, 131
History of, 3–4
Historic sites, basic information, 132
Honesty, significance of, 189
Horseback riding, basic information, 132
Hospitals, basic information, 132
Hotel and Travel Guide, information provided, 80, 176
Hotel brochures/advertising, necessary supply of, 34
Hotels
    basic information, 132
    reservation services provided, 80–81
Housekeeping department
    responsibilities of, 19
    standards of, 167

I

Ice cream shops, recommendations for, 133
Ice skating, information regarding, 133
In-house services, *see specific services*

Interviews
    handling of, 224–226
    preparation tips, 223
Introduction to guest, types of, 53, 104–105,
    166, 211

J
Jazz, current information regarding, 133

K
Kennels, information regarding, 133

L
Lentz, Dilys, 232
Libraries, basic information, 134
Limousines, providing, 82–83, 134
Liquor stores, basic information, 134
Locker space, size requirements, 35–36
Logbook
    package delivery, 173
    required information, 68–72
    restaurant reservation requests, 87
    theater tickets requests, 93
Lost and found departments, basic information, 135
Luggage storage, provision for, 35

M
Mail
    handling procedures, 163–164
    organization of, 35
    questions regarding, 50
    space provided for, 35
Main lobby services, 33
Management, relationship with, 17–18. *See also*
    specific departments

Managing Director, duties of, 15
Maps
    atlas availability, 172
    direction assistance, 50–51
    supply of, 34, 174
Marriage licenses, information regarding, 135
Massages, scheduling procedure, 97, 135
Messages for guests, computerized system, 64
Messenger services, providing, 135, 173–174
Medical/scientific convention groups, assisting, 45
Miscellaneous charge form, function of, 65–66
Money machines, availability information, 136
Motels, basic information, 136
Movie theaters, current information, 136
Museums, information regarding, 105, 136–138, 141
Music, information regarding, 138

N
Networking
    importance of, 25–26
    startup of, 63
New business, creation of, 109
Newsstand, basic information, 138
Nightlife, current information, *see specific activity*
Notary public, availability of, 138

O
Observation, on-the-job training and, 73
Observation decks, basic information, 139
Observatories, basic information, 139
Official Airlines Guide, use of, 77–79
Off-track betting (OTB), basic information, 138–139
On-the-job training, basics of, 63
Opera, current information, 139
Organization skills, significance of, 7
Out-of-house services, *see specific service*

P

Package handling procedures, 164–165
Paid-out form, function of, 64–65
Parks, information regarding, 139
Passports, assistance with, 140
Personality skills, significance of, 7–8, 189
Photocopying services, availability of, 175–176
Piano bars, current information, 140
Piers, basic information, 140
Pizza, information regarding, 141
Planetariums, basic information, 141
Polo, information regarding, 141
Post offices, basic information, 141
Postal information
    current rates, 141
    scale availability, 174
    zip code directory, 176
Professional case stories, 231–236
Public relations, significance of, 201

Q

Qualifications, 7–8
Questions, responding to, 47–49

R

Racetracks, information regarding, 142
Radio car service, providing, 83–84, 142
Radio stations, information regarding, 142
Railroad service
    information regarding, 142
    reservations, 84
Reader Board, oversights, 24
Records/tapes, shopping information, 143
Reference materials, necessary supply of, 34
Religious services, questions regarding, 50
Repair services, information regarding, 146

Reputation, establishment of, 48, 193
Research of guests/companies, process of, 54–56
Reservations, questions regarding, 50
Reservations department, working with, 19, 109
Resident Manager
    duties of, 15, 17
    working with, 109
Restaurant Management, relationship with, 22–23
Restaurant reservations
    ethics involved, 90
    required information, 86–88, 104
Restaurants
    importance to, 22–23
    recommendations, 85, 88–90, 147, 182
Return business, generation of, 19, 44, 46, 109,
    166, 188
Rock n' Roll, basic information, 148
Room inspections, assistance with, 18, 20, 167
Room service
    order form, function of, 66–67
    role of, 214
    working with, 23–24

S

Salary issues, 5
Sales/Marketing department, working with,
    25–26, 109
Secretarial services
    information regarding, 148
    providing, 97
Security department
    relationship with, 21
    working with, 9–10
Security guards, rental information, 148
Self-education, significance of, 103–108
Ships, basic information, 148

Shoe shine, basic information, 149
Shopping centers/malls, information regarding, 50, 149
Showing rooms, procedure of, 168–169
Sightseeing, information regarding, 149. *See also specific topics of interest*
Sightseeing tours
    booking procedure, 94–95
    information regarding, 155, 175
Singles' bars, current information, 150
Skyscrapers, basic information, 150
Special occasions, handling of, 24
Sporting events, obtaining tickets for, 94, 155
Sporting goods, shopping information, 150
Sports bars, basic information, 150
Squares addresses, information regarding, 150
Stadiums, information regarding, 151
Staff, duties of, 208
Stationery, supply of, 35
Steyger, Ben, 236
Storage, space requirements, 34–36, 206
Stores/shopping, basic information, 151
Street guide, location information, 151
Strollers, rental services and, 145–146
Subways systems, information regarding, 151–152
Supervisor, role of, 208

T
Tailors, listing of, 152
Taxis
    complaints regarding, 152
    listing of, 152
Tearooms/service, information regarding, 153
Telegrams, listing for, 153
Telephone
    dialing information, 174
    introduction call, 53

Telephone directory, as information source, 106, 109, 130, 132, 144–146, 152-153
Telephone manner, development of, 72–73, 104–105
Telephone numbers, listing of, 153
Television shows
    obtaining tickets for, 90–91
    studio information, 153
Telex
    availability information, 153
    providing of service, 174
Tennis, court information, 154
Theaters
    listing of, 154
    ticket reservation process, 91–94, 104
Ticket services, dealing with, 90–94
Time zone information, 155
Tipping
    amount of, 183
    customary service of, 181–182
    pooling of, 183
    sources of, 46
Titled guests, treatment of, 58
Tobacco, shopping information, 155
Tops of building information, *see* Observation decks
Tourist information service, referral to, 155
Tours, *see* Sightseeing tours
Towed cars, retrieval information, 156
Toys, shopping information, 156
Trade show exhibitors/attendees convention groups, assisting, 44
Travel agency service, information regarding, 156
Tunnels, location information, 157
Twenty-four-hour activities, current information, 157

U
United Service Organization (USO), information regarding, 157

V

van der Vloed, Barbara, 234
Veterinarians, listing of, 157
VIPs
    bodyguard rental, 148
    identification of, 56
    special requests by, 57–58
    treatment of, 56–57, 167

W

Welcome notes, introduction by, 53

Y

Yachts, information regarding, 157–158

Z

Ziminski, Adele, 231–232
Zoos, basic information, 158